How to use *explore*

Issue 110

The 91 daily readings in this issue of *Explore* are designed to help you understand and apply the Bible as you read it each day.

It's serious!

We suggest that you allow 15 minutes each day to work through the Bible passage with the notes. It should be a meal, not a snack! Readings from other parts of the Bible can throw valuable light on the study passage. These cross-references can be skipped if you are already feeling full up, but will expand your grasp of the Bible. *Explore* uses the NIV2011 Bible translation, but you can also use it with the NIV1984 or ESV translations.

Sometimes a prayer box will encourage you to stop and pray through the lessons—but it is always important to allow time to pray for God's Spirit to bring his word to life, and to shape the way we think and live through it.

We're serious!

All of us who work on *Explore* share a passion for getting the Bible into people's lives. We fiercely hold to the Bible as God's word—to honour and follow, not to explain away.

1 Find a time you can read the Bible each day

2 Find a place where you can be quiet and think

3 Ask God to help you understand

4 Carefully read through the Bible passage for today

5 Study the verses with *Explore*, taking time to think

6 Pray about what you have read

thegoodbook
COMPANY

BIBLICAL | RELEVANT | ACCESSIBLE

Welcome to *explore*

Being a Christian isn't a skill you learn, nor is it a lifestyle choice. It's about having a real relationship with the living God through his Son, Jesus Christ. The Bible tells us that this relationship is like a marriage.

It's important to start with this, because it is easy to view the practice of daily Bible reading as a Christian duty, or a hard discipline that is just one more thing to get done in our busy lives.

But the Bible is God speaking to us: opening his mind to us on how he thinks, what he wants for us and what his plans are for the world. And most importantly, it tells us what he has done for us in sending his Son, Jesus Christ, into the world. It's the way that the Spirit shows Jesus to us, and changes us as we behold his glory.

Here are a few suggestions for making your time with God more of a joy than a burden:

- *Time:* Find a time when you will not be disturbed. Many people have found that the morning is the best time as it sets you up for the day. But whatever works for you is right for you.

- *Place:* Jesus says that we are not to make a great show of our religion (see Matthew 6:5-6), but rather, to pray with the door to our room shut. Some people plan to get to work a few minutes earlier and get their Bible out in an office or some other quiet corner.

- *Prayer:* Although *Explore* helps with specific prayer ideas from the passage, do try to develop your own lists to pray through. Use the flap inside the back cover to help with this. And allow what you read in the Scriptures to shape what you pray for yourself, the world and others.

- *Feast:* You can use the "Bible in a year" line at the bottom of each page to help guide you through the entire Scriptures throughout 2025. This year, each day explores a different genre of the Bible. On Sundays, you'll read from a New Testament epistle; on Mondays, from the first five books of the Bible ("the Law"); Tuesdays cover Old Testament history books; Wednesdays enjoy the Psalms and Thursdays Old Testament poetry; Fridays focus on the prophets, and then on Saturdays you'll read through the Gospels. You can find the original version at bible-reading.com/bible-plan/html.

- *Share:* As the saying goes, *expression deepens impression.* So try to cultivate the habit of sharing with others what you have learned. Why not join our Facebook group to share your encouragements, questions and prayer requests? Search for *Explore: For your daily walk with God.*

And enjoy it! As you read God's word and God's Spirit works in your mind and your heart, you are going to see Jesus, and appreciate more of his love for you and his promises to you. That's amazing!

Carl Laferton is the Editorial Director of The Good Book Company

JOSHUA: Promised land

Joshua is a book about courage, strength and security. Sounds good? It's also a book about being radical, obedient and uncompromising.

And more than that, it's a book about the God who is perfect, powerful and promise-keeping.

Since Joshua picks up the story where Deuteronomy leaves it, we begin at the end of the previous book…

Read Deuteronomy 34

❓ *Where is Moses (v 1-3)?*

❓ *What is exciting about what he can see (v 4)?*

❓ *What note of tragedy is there (v 4)?*

Moses had, in God's strength, brought the Israelites out of Egypt and led them through the desert. He had, with God's guidance, given them God's law, and pleaded with God for them when they sinned. Now he was dead.

Imagine you're an Israelite standing on the edge of the land. It's full of enemies. And your great leader has died.

❓ *How would you feel?*

❓ *How might verse 4 and verse 9 give you some hope?*

Read Joshua 1:1-5

❓ *What will God do (v 2, 3-4, 5)?*

❓ *What must Joshua do (v 2)?*

These are outrageous promises! God is describing a huge area of land, full of pow- erful city-kings and people groups. But God points Joshua to the fact that he'd promised this land to Moses (v 3). When he'd done

that, Israel were slaves under the boot of a superpower, Egypt (Exodus 3:7-10). Before that, he had promised it to Abraham, as he'd reminded Moses (Deuteronomy 34:4). When he'd done that, Abraham had been a childless nomad. Yet here his descendants were, numerous and free, on the edge of the promised land.

There was much to do before the land was Israel's. Yet the land was already Israel's. God had promised it to them. And, as he was reminding Moses and Joshua, God does what he says he'll do. Which is one of the themes of the book of Joshua: God keeps his promises.

⌄ Apply

"In keeping with his promise we are looking forward to a new heaven and a new earth, where righteousness dwells" (2 Peter 3:13). The ultimate promised land still lies before us.

❓ *Does anything ever make you doubt you'll get there?*

Remember that your future relies on God's promise! Joshua could look back to God's promise-keeping rescue from Egypt through Moses—and we can look back to God's promise-keeping rescue from death through the Lord Jesus. We know that what God has promised, he does!

❓ *How does this expel your doubts?*

Bible in a year: 1 Samuel 11 – 15

Living by the promises

God keeps his promises. So how will knowing this truth affect his people?.

Read Joshua 1:6-9

God's promises

❷ *What promises does God make here?*

❷ *Many of them are repeating what God had told Joshua in verses 1-5. Why does he repeat himself, do you think?*

God's people

❷ *What is the repeated phrase here?*

Each time this phrase comes up, God gives Joshua reasons why he should, and can, act in this way.

❷ *What are the reasons (v 6, 9)?*

❷ *Between these phrases, God tells Joshua to do something else. What is it (v 7-8)?*

⌄ Apply

❷ *Do verses 7-8 describe your attitude to God's word?*

❷ *How could you "meditate" on it more often?*

❷ *How could you be more "careful to do everything written in it"?*

❷ *What motivations do these verses give you to study, speak, remember and obey God's word?*

Verses 7-8 show us what God means by being "strong and courageous". It's not about physical strength. It isn't about never experiencing terror. It's about feeling weak and out of our

depth, and yet still remembering, loving and obeying how God tells us to live—because we know God keeps his promises.

Looking back

Read Joshua 23:1-11

By now, Joshua is "a very old man" (v 1).

❷ *What has God done for his people under Joshua's leadership (v 1, 3, 9-10)?*

❷ *What will he continue to do (v 5)?*

❷ *How should his people respond to his promise (v 6-8, 11)?*

Throughout the book of Joshua, we'll see God's people acting with strength and courage, because they trust God to keep his promises. (We'll also see them failing to do so when they forget his promises.) Again and again, Joshua will teach us: God keeps his promises—so be strong and courageous in obeying him.

···· TIME OUT ·····································

Throughout the Scriptures, love for God (v 11) and uncompromising obedience to God (v 6-7) are two sides of the same coin. If we love God, we will obey him; because obeying God is how we love him. **Read John 14:23-24**.

❷ *It's worth asking ourselves: is my obedience grudging or loving? Does my love produce obedience or complacency?*

Restful fighting

Israel are camped east of the Jordan, ready to cross into enemy territory and make it their home. Except that some of them are already home.

Two and a half of the twelve tribes had been allocated land east of the river. (See Numbers 32.)

Rest

Read Joshua 1:10-13

❓ *How has God given the Reubenites, Gadites and half of the Manassites "rest" (v 13)?*

Centuries later, Solomon would sum up what "rest" means: "no adversary or disaster" (1 Kings 5:4). To enjoy rest is to enjoy blessing, to experience life under God's rule in God's world.

❓ *Why might the command of Joshua 1:10-11 not seem really to apply to these tribes?*

Fight

Read Joshua 1:14-15

❓ *What does Joshua tell the men who already have "rest" to do?*

❓ *How long are they to do this for (v 15)?*

❓ *Why might it have been tempting for these men to say "no" to Joshua?*

These men were already enjoying God's blessing in a way that their brothers weren't. But they were still asked to "cross over ahead of your fellow Israelites". Enjoying God's blessing is not a reason to retire happily to the sidelines of church life; it frees us to give all we can in service of struggling brothers and sisters. An area of life where God has made things go well for us is an area where he gives us the opportunity to help others into his blessing.

This is, of course, radically challenging to our me-first culture (and hearts). Church is not there to meet our needs; we are there to meet others' needs. There are times when we need others to put themselves out for us, getting alongside us as we struggle; there are times we should be taking the strain for others.

▼ Apply

❓ *How does this view of church life encourage you and challenge you?*

Be strong

Read Joshua 1:16-18

❓ *How do these men respond?*

❓ *What is their encouragement to Joshua (end of v 18)?*

▼ Apply

❓ *When was the last time you encouraged a fellow Christian to be strong and courageous in obeying the promise-keeping God?*

❓ *Who needs you to encourage them in this way today?*

Bible in a year: Job 25 –26

The faithful prostitute

She turns up to your church service late, straight from working in the red-light district. Meet Rahab, one of the heroines of Bible history.

Read Joshua 2:1-24

Protected

We don't know why the two Israelite spies end up at a prostitute's house (v 1). But they're found out; and the king orders them to be handed over (v 3).

❓ *What's the obvious thing for Rahab, a citizen of Jericho, to do at this point?*

❓ *What does she actually do (v 4-7)? Where does her loyalty clearly lie?*

The prostitute's God

Why would Rahab risk everything to protect two men who have come to spy out her city so they can conquer it?!

❓ *What answer do verses 9-13 give?*

❓ *Why has Rahab transferred her loyalties from the king of Jericho to the Lord of Israel?*

Rahab knows that God will win. And she knows that she lies on the wrong side, in the path of his victory.

❓ *What does she need (v 13)?*

Protection

❓ *What do the men know God will do (v 14)?*

❓ *What do they promise Rahab (v 14, 17-20)?*

☑ Apply

❓ *How do we see people in this passage acting courageously because they know God keeps his promises?*

❓ *What comforts and security do you risk in order to live for God?*

What the spies promised to do, they did (6:20-25). Rahab trusted God's promises. She trusted God's people's promises. And she was saved to enjoy life among God's people. Not only that but God used her to further his plan to bring his Son into the world (see Matthew 1:1-17, especially verse 5).

The book of Joshua will see much death and devastation as Israel conquers Canaan. Rahab serves as a reminder that no one is beyond God's forgiveness. No one need face destruction. Anyone can recognise God, cry out for salvation, and come into his people to be used for his purposes.

···· TIME OUT ································

❓ *Would a prostitute in your area think she would find a welcome at your church on Sunday? Why/why not?*

☑ Apply

The spies knew God keeps his promises; and they kept their own promise to Rahab. Keeping our word is God-like.

❓ *Are you known as someone who will go to great lengths to keep your promises?*

Into the land

At a distance of over 3,000 years, it's easy to miss the significance of what happens in our section today.

The headline, in a way, isn't so much *how* God brings his people through the River Jordan, but rather *where* he brings them to—the promised land.

Read all of Joshua 3 – 4

> ❷ *Sum up in a couple of sentences what happens. (If you like, you could sketch it.)*
>
> ❷ *What particularly strikes you about God from this passage?*

Since it's a long section to read, we'll just pick out a couple of aspects of it here.

Know the way

The "ark of the covenant" (3:3) was the gold-lined box in which God chose to live among his people.

> ❷ *What wouldn't the people be able to know, left to themselves (3:4)?*
>
> ❷ *So what did they need to do (v 3-4)?*

The image of God's people entering this promised land is often used as a picture of believers entering the eternal promised land. None of us have ever set foot there. The way to it is through death, and is a route we have never travelled. But, like Israel, we have simply to keep our eye on God's presence. Jesus, God himself made flesh, assures us that: "I am the way" (John 14:6). He promises to "come back and take you to be with me" (v 3).

⌃ Pray

"When I tread the verge of Jordan,
　Bid my anxious fears subside;
Death of death, and hell's destruction,
　Land me safe on Canaan's side.
Songs of praises, songs of praises,
I will ever give to thee; I will ever give to thee."

Prepare for God

> ❷ *What do the people need to do (Joshua 3:5)?*
>
> ❷ *What about the priests (v 6, 8)?*

"Consecrate" means "prepare" or "be ready". It's not until verse 13 that we discover what God is going to do. But even before they find out, the Israelites are to be prepared, watching with anticipation to see what God will do. The priests are to be obedient to the command of God's chosen leader, even though Joshua's words must have sounded strange!

⌄ Apply

The Christian life is not about obeying God when we can see what he's up to. It's about obeying him while we wait to see what he's up to. It's about living in anticipation that we will see God doing great things for us, in us and through us.

> ❷ *Is this how you live each day? In what ways could you do this more fully?*
>
> ❷ *How do the events of Joshua 3 – 4 encourage you to get on with it?*

Bible in a year: Mark 5 – 6

Neither fight nor flee

Can you recall a time when you were utterly overwhelmed by problems and could see no possible way out? What did you do?

If I had wings…

Read Psalm 55:1-8

❓ *What is happening?*

David was a mighty warrior who fearlessly faced down the giant Goliath. But…

❓ *What does he wish he could do (v 8)?*

The sum of all fears

Read Psalm 55:9-15

❓ *Where does David face danger?*

❓ *Who is his enemy here?*

The events of 9/11 were terrifying because the great skyscrapers that crumbled before our eyes were such emblems of our security. Likewise, the means of their destruction were not fighter jets but passenger planes, which we use to go on holiday, for business travel, or to see distant family. This shattering of security is what David is facing: the city was the place of safety and security in ancient times, and close friends are the people he (and we) should be able to trust above all else.

So when we read in verse 9 that there is "violence and strife in the city", and in verses 12-13 that it is David's "close friend" who has betrayed him, we realise that the rug really has been pulled from under his feet.

The God I can trust

Read Psalm 55:16-23

The verses move back and forth between God and David's enemies.

❓ *What does David know that God will do for him if he calls on him?*

❓ *This section is bracketed by verses 16 and 23. What is David's resolution?*

Both verses declare his commitment, his trust in God. It's easy to overlook the little phrase at the start of verse 16—"as for me". He has seen his closest godly friend turn away from God, but he refuses to give up on God. He will keep on trusting.

Jesus taught that the psalms pointed to his own sufferings (Luke 24:26-27, 44). So this psalm gives insight into what it felt like for Jesus to be betrayed by his "close friend" (Psalm 55:13)—**read Matthew 26:20-25, 45-50.**

❓ *How does this help you think more deeply about Jesus' sufferings?*

⌃ Pray

Fight or flight? When people turn against you, how do you respond? David the warrior wished he could fly away. But the right response is neither lashing out nor running off; it is calling on and trusting in the Lord.

"Cast your cares on the LORD and he will sustain you; he will never let the righteous be shaken" (Psalm 55:22).

❓ *What cares do you need to unburden yourself of today?*

 Bible in a year: 1 Corinthians 11 – 12

A glimpse of heaven

God's people are in God's land. What is life like there?

The outward sign

Read Joshua 5:1-9

We sometimes hear of mass baptisms; here's a mass circumcision (v 2-3), so big that the place was named after the event.

> ❷ *Why did these people need circumcising (v 5)?*
> ❷ *Why had their circumcised fathers not entered the promised land (v 6)?*

God had told Abraham and all his male descendants to be circumcised as an outward sign of their internal loyalty and obedience to God (see Genesis 17).

> ❷ *How does this passage in Joshua remind us what circumcision didn't guarantee? (Think about the circumcised generation of Joshua 5:5-6.)*

An inward attitude of faithful obedience was what brought people into the land. That attitude was shown externally by circumcision; but circumcision itself did not prove that the attitude existed. God blessed the uncircumcised, obedient generation, but judged their circumcised, unfaithful fathers.

···· TIME OUT ····

Most Christians agree that there are some parallels between Old Testament circumcision and New Testament baptism.

> ❷ *How does Joshua 5 shape our understanding of why baptism is important, and why it's not all-important?*

The remembrance meal

Read Joshua 5:10

The Passover meal helped Israel remember that God kept his promises and saved his people from his judgment.

> ❷ *Why was it appropriate that they celebrated this as they entered his land?*

···· TIME OUT ····

Read Matthew 26:26-29

Jesus redefined the Passover meal as pointing to his death.

> ❷ *Where will it be shared (v 29)?*

We'll always share the Lord's Supper. For now, we take it on the journey. One day, we'll share it face to face with Jesus, in the promised land, looking back to how he delivered us from slavery and brought us to his kingdom. A wonderful prospect!

Enjoyment of blessings

Read Joshua 5:11-12

God had fed Israel miraculous bread from heaven throughout their time in the desert. Now, he stops.

> ❷ *So how do they get food?*

We experience God's provision for us daily, physically and spiritually. But the blessings we enjoy now will be dwarfed by the blessings that lie ahead of us.

Bible in a year: Exodus 1 – 4

On our side?

In the American Civil War, a minister told US President Abraham Lincoln that he hoped God was on their side.

Lincoln's response was cutting, and biblical: "Sir, my concern is not whether God is on our side; my greatest concern is to be on God's side, for God is always right".

Whose side are you on?

Read Joshua 5:13 – 6:1

The Israelites have crossed into Canaan; now they're outside one of its greatest cities. It's a siege; and it's a stalemate between Israel and Jericho (6:1). But there's another army ready to fight, too...

- ❷ *Whose army (5:14)?*
- ❷ *Why does Joshua's question in verse 13 seem sensible?*
- ❷ *How does the answer in verse 14 show the inadequacy of the question?*

Joshua tries again in verse 14! This time, he simply asks what God's army commander wants to say to him.

- ❷ *What is the answer (v 15)?*

···· TIME OUT ·····································

Read Exodus 3:3-6

- ❷ *Who is present in the burning bush?*
- ❷ *What does Moses have to do in recognition of who it is?*
- ❷ *So, what is the commander of the Lord's army telling Joshua in Joshua 5:15?*

This must have been a humbling moment for God's chosen leader, in charge of a huge army. God was not on his side! The commander of God's army had come to fight not for Joshua but for God. What mattered was not Joshua's cause or plans but God's. And what mattered was that Joshua was on God's side.

▼ Apply

Think about your day: your plans, hopes and ambitions. Think about your life: your plans, hopes and ambitions for it.

- ❷ *Are you asking God to be on your side, delivering all that you want your life to be? Or are you asking God to make sure you are on his side, whatever changes that means for your plans and hopes?*

The winning side

Read Joshua 6:2-21

- ❷ *Why is the outcome certain from verse 2 onwards?*
- ❷ *How does the way that Jericho falls clearly demonstrate which army it is that wins this victory?*

▲ Pray

Heavenly Father, thank you that you are infinitely powerful, and so can keep all your promises. Help me today not to expect you to be on my side but humbly to seek to be on yours. Would your will be done, even when it is different to mine. Amen.

Bible in a year: 1 Samuel 16 – 20

Is this genocide?

Hostile atheists sometimes argue that passages such as Joshua 6 are promoting genocide. And our own hearts, too, often feel troubled by what is happening here.

Since this is history, it can't be explained away as myth. Since God is unchanging, the God we worship now is the one who commanded this killing then. How do we respond to the destruction of Canaan?

Destruction deserved

Read Leviticus 18:3, 20-28

❓ *What do we learn here about the lifestyle of the people who lived in Canaan?*

❓ *What is particularly horrific about v 21?*

Read Deuteronomy 9:4-6

❓ *What were the Israelites not able to claim, as they took the land?*

❓ *Why are the nations in the land being destroyed (v 4)?*

❓ *Why is Israel given the land (end v 5)?*

The residents of Jericho were not morally neutral; they were "wicked"—in rebellion against God and against his ways. They had chosen to live in defiance of him. They were wicked—but they were also no worse than us. In a sense, you and I and everyone are inhabitants of Jericho, "filled with every kind of wickedness" (Romans 1:29). It may reveal itself differently but we, too, naturally choose to live in God's world in defiance of him.

In this specific period of history, Israel's role was to act as bailiffs, evicting tenants who had committed murder on God's property. One day, all people will face a final, and fair, eviction at God's hands.

Destruction delivered

Read Joshua 6:15-27

❓ *How do the events here link back to what we've seen in Leviticus and Deuteronomy?*

❓ *Imagine that Joshua, or Israel as a whole, had decided not to destroy Jericho. What would they have been saying about God?*

Delivered from destruction

❓ *What does the writer of Joshua seem keen to point out to us in verses 17, 22-23, 25?*

This woman was a prostitute. She was de-filed. But she was saved, because she asked for rescue. The shock of Joshua 6 isn't that the inhabitants of Jericho were judged and killed, but that one resident wasn't.

And the shock of the whole Bible is not that God judges people, but that he is the "God who justifies the ungodly" (Romans 4:5). God's judgment is deserved; his rescue isn't. But still he offers it.

Pray

Thank God that he cares enough about his world to judge and destroy those who ruin it. Thank him that he cares enough about us to provide a way of salvation through his Son. Thank him for saving you.

Take and give

God brought his people into the land, and gave them Jericho. Joshua, full of courage as he trusts God to keep his promises, begins to plan the next stage of conquest...

Disaster

Read Joshua 7:2-9

❷ *This is land God has promised to give to Israel. Why are these events such a surprise?*

❷ *How does Joshua react (v 6-9)?*

···· TIME OUT ····································

What does Joshua care about most? Not himself, or the people but God and his glory. If Israel's defeat becomes known, and is repeated, "what then will you do for your own great name?" (v 9).

God's reputation and honour should be our greatest ambition. It's why we're taught to begin praying by saying, "Hallowed be your name, your kingdom come, your will be done".

Disclosure

Read Joshua 7:1, 10-23

❷ *Why was Israel defeated at Ai (v 1, 10-12)?*

For this, "the Lord's anger burned against Israel" (v 1). But what was so serious about Achan's sin? It was a breaking of the covenant (v 15). God had promised to provide land and blessing for his people; his people were committed to obeying him. But Achan had sought to grasp the plunder of the land for himself, and therefore disobeyed God. Rather than trust God to give, he had opted to take. Coveting (v 21) is covenant-breaking.

⌄ Apply

We need to check our own hearts. I need to ask myself, am I trusting God to give me all I need, and therefore obeying him even when that costs me or am I trusting myself to gain all I want for myself, and so disobeying God when it is convenient?

Death

Read Joshua 7:24-26

This may seem harsh. But "the wages of sin is death" (Romans 6:23). Exclusion from God's blessings (including life) is the punishment for seeking to grab blessings ourselves.

Dominance

Read Joshua 8:1-8 (or if you have time, to v 29)

❷ *What should Joshua not be? Why (v 1-2)?*

It's the theme of Joshua: God keeps his promises, so be strong and courageous in obeying him. Achan decided not to obey, and so did not enjoy the fulfilment of God's promises.

❷ *What does God tell Israel they may do (v 2)?*

God pours blessings out on his obedient people as he keeps his promises. The lesson of Achan's sin is: don't try to grasp for yourself what God stands ready to freely give. You don't need to!

 Bible in a year: Job 27 – 28

Welcome to today's service

We're pausing briefly from watching Israel in battle to listen in on Israel at "church".

Read Joshua 8:30-35

Where?

Places have significance. The Falklands is not just a group of islands in British minds. Gettysburg means more than simply a town to Americans.

❷ *Where does Joshua's service take place (v 30, 33)?*

❷ *What does he build there (v 30)?*

At the foot of these mountains was the town of Shechem.

Read Genesis 12:1-7

Now, five centuries after Genesis 12, Abram's offspring are gathered in the land, at Shechem, around an altar.

❷ *What statement was Joshua making by choosing this place?*

❷ *How would the people have felt as they gathered there, do you think?*

What?

❷ *What happens at this service:*
  • *Joshua 8:31?*
  • *v 32, 34-35?*

The sacrificial system was the way imperfect Israel could remain in relationship with their perfect God. The commands of the Book of the Law (the first five books of our Bible) were the way forgiven Israel were to live out their relationship with their merciful God.

Who?

❷ *What do you think is significant about the details that the congregation included...*
  • *foreigners (v 33, 35—i.e. people not biologically descended from Abram)?*
  • *children (v 35)?*

Apply

At times of great blessing for God's people, God's law is valued, read and obeyed (e.g. Nehemiah 8:5-12).

❷ *What is your attitude to God's word? Are there ways you're wanting God's blessings without obeying him?*

Four piles of stones

The altar in Joshua 8:30-31 is the fourth pile of stones built since God's people crossed the Jordan, each intended to remind Israel who God is and how to obey him:

• 4:1-7, to remember the River Jordan parting: *God gives his people victory.*

• 7:24-26, to remember Achan's sin: *God's people need to obey him.*

• 8:28-29, to remember the king of Ai's death: *God defeats his enemies.*

• 8:30-31, to remember the gathering at Shechem: *God keeps his promises to his people.*

Foolishly fooled

Common sense is a wonderful thing... isn't it?

A cunning plan

Read Joshua 9:1-13

Israel are about to face a powerful enemy (v 1-2). But first, they face a cunning one.

Gibeon is just 15 miles from Jericho—part of the land God had told his people to conquer. But God had also told Israel that they could make treaties with people who lived outside the land he was giving them (Deuteronomy 20:10-18).

❷ *How do the Hivites (who live in Gibeon) fool Israel? What is their aim?*

❷ *How is this a common-sense approach?*

Falling for it

Read Joshua 9:14-15

The Israelites are suspicious (v 7).

❷ *How do they work out whether to believe the men from Gibeon?*

❷ *What don't they do?*

❷ *What decision do they make?*

They use their common sense. Their logic. Their reason. And they get it wrong. Self-reliance is not a Christian quality. Yet how often I forget God's word because the answer to a question or decision just seems so obvious! Perhaps it's not so much in the difficult decisions of life, but rather in the apparently easy ones, that it's easy to rely on common sense rather than God's perfect guidance.

TIME OUT

❷ *Looking over last week, is there anything significant that you've done or decided that you didn't pray about?*

❷ *Why didn't you?*

Living with it

Read Joshua 9:16-27

The Israelites realise they've been conned (v 16)—but it's too late!

❷ *Why don't they just attack anyway (v 18-20)?*

My parents used to tell me: two wrongs don't make a right. Here, Israel has made a mistake because they relied on themselves instead of praying to the Lord. But Joshua refuses to do the wrong thing (break a covenant) in order to make good a previous wrong thing.

The life of a flawed Christian (you and me!) is often about living with the consequences of decisions we regret. Joshua reminds us that while we cannot change the mistakes of yesterday, and while we must live with them, we can make sure we do the godly thing today.

⌃ Pray

"Trust in the LORD with all your heart and lean not on your own understanding; in all your ways submit to him, and he will make your paths straight" (Proverbs 3:5-6). Pray about your day—all of it!

EASTER: Questions

The Lord Jesus was brilliant at answering the questions people put to him. But this Easter, we're going to look at eight searching questions that he asked others...

Opposition to the Lord started early in his public ministry. And it came from the last two places you might expect: from the religious leaders—who should have welcomed the long-awaited Messiah, and from his family. We pick up John's story as Jesus goes to Jerusalem after he has performed the miraculous feeding of the crowds by the lake.

Read John 7:14-18

❓ *There is delicious irony in the question from the Jewish leaders in verse 15. Why do you think they are surprised?*

❓ *What does Jesus' answer in verses 16-18 make plain to them?*

Hatred

The leaders grumble that Jesus hasn't got the right qualifications, hasn't been to the right college, and yet he seems to be able to teach the Bible better than them! Not surprising if you understand that the eternal Word is the author and subject of the written word—the Bible.

❓ *Why would Jesus' answer have challenged and threatened the Jewish teachers?*

Murderers

Read John 7:19-20

❓ *What question does Jesus pose (v 19)?*

The law of Moses makes clear that murdering an innocent person is unlawful (Exodus 20:13).

❓ *So why is Jesus' statement (John 7:19) such a shock?*

❓ *How do the crowd respond (v 20)?*

Criticism is often expressed in polite terms—especially when it comes from public figures with reputations and positions to maintain. But underneath the flattery—underneath the polite question—there is deep-rooted anger and, increasingly, murderous hatred.

⌄ Apply

Jesus' miracles, claims and teaching will always provoke the same reactions. People will smile in pity at you or dismiss you (and your Lord) with faint praise.

❓ *Have you experienced this kind of "gentle hostility" towards your own faith, or perhaps to your church? What does this incident suggest may be going on underneath—even among your friends?*

❓ *Is there anything to learn from the way the Lord Jesus confronts his opponents?*

⌃ Pray

Thank Jesus for being the heaven-sent, God-honouring teacher. Pray that you would, like him, have courage to stand up for the truth; and the confidence to ask questions which draw out other people's heart-attitudes.

Are you still sleeping?

After Jesus' last, emotional meal with his friends, Judas departed to betray him. What had been predicted for millennia had started to unfold.

Dark night...

Read Matthew 26:36-45

❷ *How does the Lord describe his state of mind in verse 38?*

❷ *Why might he want the disciples to "keep watch" with him?*

Have you ever spent time with someone who is "sorrowful to the point of death"? Perhaps you have felt something like it yourself? If so, you will know how desperate and crushing it can feel to be so overwhelmed by a tragedy such as the loss of someone close to you, or the pain of a broken relationship. If you're a friend of someone going through a dark time, it may be that your concerned presence is the only thing you can give. It is what the Lord asks of his friends here.

... of the soul

Re-read Matthew 26:39

"This cup" is Jesus' forthcoming suffering on the cross.

❷ *Read Isaiah 51:17. What exactly is this suffering?*

❷ *Why would it make him "overwhelmed with sorrow to the point of death"?*

❷ *What does he pray?*

The sleepers

Re-read Matthew 26:40-45

Three times, they fall asleep!

❷ *What reasons are given for why the disciples could not stay awake?*

❷ *How do you read the words that the Lord says to them? Do you think he is angry, disappointed, upset or something else?*

❷ *What do his encouragements show about what the disciples had failed to understand?*

Their fatigue is understandable. It was the middle of the night; they had been through an exhausting week of intrigue, arguments and growing hostility; they had just finished an emotional meal. But this was the moment they could have offered some support to their Lord, who prayed alone with the crushing burden of what was to follow. Not merely the physical pain of the cross but the hell of separation from his Father. He would hang on a cross for them; they could not stay awake for him.

⏷ Pray

Through their lack of understanding and weakness they were unable to do something wonderful for their Lord. Pray through some crucial things we must keep alert about in 1 Peter 5:8-9 and 1 Timothy 4:16.

Who is it you want?

His prayers are finished. His mind is settled on what will follow. Watch in awe as the Son of God, our Saviour, walks his path, determined to love us to the end.

Protecting love

Read John 18:2-11

❓ *What do verses 2-3 suggest about the party that arrived to arrest the Lord?*

❓ *Why does John list what they were carrying, do you think?*

It's an intimidating group: a traitor, soldiers, and some elite leaders. Light, noise and the metallic clank of weapons replaced the darkness and silence. Anyone would be cowed into silence and inactivity by this aggressive group with a determined purpose.

❓ *What does the Lord Jesus do (v 4)?*

❓ *What does the verse suggest is the reason he took the initiative?*

❓ *What do verses 8-9 add to the picture?*

Even as he is about to be arrested, Jesus' first thought is for his friends. He protects them from the hate being unleashed against him.

Sovereign love

❓ *How does the group respond to Jesus (v 6)?*

❓ *Who is in control here?*

Do you see the irony of this account? Notice that *he knows everything that would happen to him* (v 4). They thought their secret plans had surprised him. Not at all. *He was ready for them.* He had prepared himself thoroughly, and his disciples as much as he

was able. *He takes the initiative:* Jesus does not wait to be challenged—it is his enemies who need challenging. Did they realise who it was they were intent on capturing? Did they know Jesus was the "I AM" (God's name, by which he reveals himself and which Jesus uses for himself in verse 5)?

We should not make the mistake of feeling sorry for the Lord Jesus as he is taken to be crucified. Here is no poor fugitive with whom the enemy have at last caught up. Here is the Son of God, with all power in his hands, willingly giving himself up to achieve God's own plans.

Forgiving love

❓ *How does Peter react (v 10)? Why is this a fair reaction to what's going on?*

❓ *How does Jesus respond (v 11)?*

❓ *Why (v 11)?*

Jesus is in control. He does not need his friends to fight for him; and he himself does not want to fight. He will fight for them, not with a sword but by following the path to the cross.

⌃ Pray

Don't forget Jesus' immense pain and suffering. But don't forget that he chose to be "led like a lamb to the slaughter" (Isaiah 53:7). Don't feel sorry for him; praise him for his infinite love.

Bible in a year: 1 Samuel 21 – 25

How then would the Scriptures be fulfilled?

Read Matthew 26:47-56

Friendship betrayed

❷ *What are some of the differences in detail between Matthew's account and John's account of the arrest (which we read yesterday)?*

❷ *What does Matthew want to draw our attention to in the way he recounts the events of that night?*

❷ *What can you detect in Jesus' statement to Judas in verse 50?*

Matthew's account is at the same time more personal (the details of Judas's betraying kiss) and more cosmic (the repeated reference to fulfilled Scripture, and the reference to angels).

A kiss is a greeting for a friend. Jesus had certainly been a great friend to Judas. And though he knows it is a kiss of death, Jesus amazingly is still extending friendship towards him. Even now, Judas can choose. Even now, he can be a true friend again.

⊻ Apply

Have you ever heard those condemning words, *"But I thought you were a Christian?"* Know for sure that there is forgiveness on offer even when we have betrayed our Saviour...

Scripture fulfilled

❷ *What does verse 53 tell us Jesus could do next?*

❷ *So why doesn't he (v 54)?*

He does not approach the cross as a victim filled with a sense of futility that it is all God's will, so there is nothing to do but be carried along in the stream of inevitability. He is actively working to display for them, and for us, solid, lasting evidence that he is the Messiah, and that his death is the centre point of all history, and the climactic fulfilment of the Old Testament Scriptures. This death, in these specific circumstances, with these details, has all already been foretold.

Jesus is no unwilling victim. At any moment, he could have called more than 12,000 angels to deliver him and slaughter the wicked men who plotted to murder the Son of God. It was a deliberate act of loving will that he did not say the word to give them what they deserved—and all done because he loved us so much. *What a Saviour!*

⊼ Pray

We need to appreciate that at every moment on his path to the cross, Jesus had the power to turn back, or turn away. As we grasp this, we come to worship him for going forward, step by painful step, to his death, out of love for us. Praise him now.

Bible in a year: Psalm 42 – 44

Why did you strike me?

The night-time arrest is followed by a midnight interrogation and trial at the home of Annas. Once again, we are meant to ask, "Who is in control here?"

Secrets and lies

Read John 18:19-24

❷ *What are they questioning Jesus about (v 19)?*

❷ *What does Jesus' reply in verses 20-21 suggest they are trying to accuse him of?*

The forms of law are clear. In a trial the prosecutors must bring witnesses to testify and accuse. The irony here is that, while the leaders are secretly plotting to kill Jesus in whatever way they can, the Lord is quite open about his teaching. He has not taught his disciples a "secret" revolutionary message while preaching something else in the open. They accuse him of hiding secrets, while they themselves are hiding their dark purpose.

Re-read John 18:22-23

❷ *What makes the official so angry that he strikes (literally, slaps) the Lord?*

❷ *What is Jesus challenging them to do in his reply in verse 23?*

We read regularly in the narratives that follow that the Lord Jesus remained silent before his accusers. But he was not totally silent. He is, in effect, demanding his rights to a fair trial. And in doing so, he is accusing his accusers of their own sin. He poses them a question with many layers of answers.

❷ *What are some of the possible answers to Jesus' question in verse 23?*

TIME OUT

Read Matthew 12:1-12

❷ *What reasons does this episode suggest the leaders have for wanting to be rid of Jesus?*

Paul recounts the same mixture of misplaced zeal and religious pride driving him to persecute Christ by persecuting his people.

Read Acts 26:9-15

⌃ Pray

It is not wrong for Christians to use their rights under the law to defend themselves; to insist on a fair trial is good and proper. But there also comes a time when, if your accusers are hardened in their purpose, it is better to remain silent.

Pray for our brothers and sisters in many parts of the world who are suffering injustice right now for their faith in Christ.

My God, my God, why have you forsaken me?

Picture the appalling scene again: Jesus hanging in agony; crowds jeering loudly; midday sun blazing down—and then...

The sun hides its face

Read Matthew 27:45-53

Blackness, coldness, fear. The darkness of God's judgment and wrath. But that wrath was not directed at the crowds...

Think of the sufferings Jesus had already endured. The betrayal, the denial, the desertion. The injustice, the scourging, the spitting, the derision, the shame. The cross itself, with all its excruciating pain. But all along, something else had been uppermost in Jesus' mind. All these gruelling experiences were overshadowed by one horrific prospect. All the time, Jesus knew that he must drink the bitter cup—and now that hell had come. The darkness of the Father's anger was on him...

The Father hides his face

Aloneness. Desolation. For those agonising hours Jesus did not enjoy his Father's fellowship, presence and support—he bore alone that colossal load of sin. He alone *could* bear it, in our place.

Read Psalm 22:1-11, slowly

❓ *What is the answer to the haunting question of Matthew 27:46?*

"Why have you forsaken me?" It was for his people that Jesus must suffer—to bear the whole punishment for our foul sins. Nothing less than the experience of hell could be sufficient—the hell of being God-forsaken, of having the wrath of the Father poured out on sin, the sin the sinless Jesus was bearing in himself.

We simply cannot understand what that was like. Infinite agony, crowded into three hours. No wonder the sun went black.

⌃ Pray

We cannot understand; but we can be amazed. And we can consider whether it was for our sins. And if we know it was, we can think about Jesus' infinite love for us, and worship him...

I sometimes think about the cross,
and shut my eyes and try to see

the cruel nails, and crown of thorns,
and Jesus crucified for me.

But, even could I see him die,
I could but see a little part

of that great love which, like a fire,
is always burning in his heart.

William Walsham How

Was it not necessary?

"The answer was staring me in the face all the time, but I just didn't see it." Has that ever happened to you?

The pieces

Read Luke 24:13-24

> ❓ *Look at verses 19-24. What are some of the massive pieces of evidence that the two disciples already know?*
>
> ❓ *Why do you think they fail to see the fairly obvious?*

"It is the third day since all this took place!" Notice the striking way that the description by the two disciples echoes the predictions that the Lord Jesus had repeatedly made about his own death and resurrection. They were using virtually the same words. And yet they had no belief or expectation that they were true.

The puzzle

Read Luke 24:25-27

> ❓ *What precisely does the Lord rebuke them for?*
>
> ❓ *Who should they have believed?*
>
> ❓ *What is the difference between being "foolish" and being "slow to believe"?*

It's intriguing that Jesus does not rebuke them for not believing in his own teaching and predictions, but for not listening to the Old Testament prophets about what would happen to the Christ. He *would* fulfil all their hopes to "redeem Israel" (v 21); and to do so, it was necessary that he should die. The cross had always been the plan.

⌄ Apply

Sometimes, our failure as disciples is foolishness—not knowing, or not bothering to know. But at other times, we know everything we need to, but are slow to believe, held back by our heartfelt fears and worries about where following the truth will lead us.

> ❓ *Which are you more prone to at the moment? How will Jesus' rebuke encourage you to do something about it?*

The solution

Read Luke 24:27-35

> ❓ *What evidence is presented to the doubting disciples, and in what order?*
>
> ❓ *What is their response to their discovery?*

They were not alone in misunderstanding the kind of kingdom that the Lord Jesus was creating—not a physical kingdom, but a spiritual one that encompassed the whole world. But as they were given the best Bible overview of all time, and as they sat at dinner with the one to whom the whole Bible points, they were given eyes to see. Everything made sense.

⌃ Pray

Thank God for giving you spiritual eyes to see the truth about the risen Jesus. Ask that the truth about Jesus' fulfilment of Scripture would make your heart burn today.

Do you love me?

Sin ruins our relationship with Christ. Peter knew Jesus had shown forgiveness to the other disciples... But what about his own shameful denial? Could even he be restored?

It's really him

Read John 21:1-14

- ❓ *What signs are there in this passage that Peter truly loves Jesus?*
- ❓ *What might be some of the fears and questions that Peter still had about his own denial of Christ during the trial?*
- ❓ *What do Jesus' actions and words show about his attitude towards the disciples?*

Notice the reverence and fear they show the Lord in verse 12—not daring even to speak or ask questions. And yet the Lord is approachable and caring in very practical ways towards them.

If you have messed up, and want to know a restored relationship with the Lord, then Jesus wants to have a one-to-one with you. It's in facing your Lord that you can find your sins put behind you.

Three questions

Read John 21:15-25

- ❓ *Why does Jesus ask Peter about the genuineness of his love three times, do you think? (Hint: read John 18:15-18, 25-27.)*

Peter was hurt that Jesus asked three times. Why? Surely all the pain and shame came flooding back as he remembered what he had done three times himself. But it was necessary pain. Yes, he did love Jesus, but

Jesus knew all the failings and weakness of that poor, changeable love. Jesus aims right at the heart. Despite the way Peter had behaved, despite his weakness and sin, there was real love for Jesus deep down. It would have been easy for Peter to serve the Lord out of guilt and shame for what he had done. But now he knows that he is completely forgiven, restored and commissioned. And so he will serve him out of love and gratitude, not guilt.

✅ Apply

Can you hear Jesus probing your heart? That love you talk about, sing about—is it really so strong, is it true love at all? How do you know if those feelings you have in church are real love for the Lord?

Read John 14:15, 23

What is your confession as you face the Lord's question: *Do you love me?* Don't avoid answering it, because he knows everything about you. Ultimately, this is the only question that matters. We cannot avoid it: but if we look at the events of that first Easter and answer: "Yes—not as much as I should, and not as much as I one day will, but yes", then we can know we are forgiven, restored, and commissioned to live for our loving Lord every day before and beyond our deaths.

- ❓ *How will this change your Easter Sunday this year, and your week next week?*

Bible in a year: 1 Corinthians 15 – 16

JOSHUA: Sun stood still

We are back in the book of Joshua. Now, the fighting really begins… and even nature will play a part.

Alliance

Read Joshua 10:1-7

Israel regretted entering a covenant with Gibeon: but, once made, they kept to it. After all, God's people understood the importance of covenants. All that they were and all that they had was a result of God keeping covenant with them; and this showed in how they helped Gibeon, undeserving though they were.

⌄ Apply

All that we are and all that we have is given to us by God who has brought us into his covenant, undeserving of his love though we are.

> ❷ *Does that show in how you keep your promises and assurances?*

Battle

Read Joshua 10:8-14

> ❷ *Why does Joshua know the result before the fighting starts (v 8)?*

> ❷ *What supernatural events in the natural world show that this is God's victory?*

···· TIME OUT ··

We rarely think of God as a warrior. But God fights, and triumphs, for his people. Which means that, though we are in a fight against spiritual opposition (Ephesians 6:10-20), we will win—not through our strength but his.

Curse

Read Joshua 10:15-27

The kings Joshua kills here (v 25-26) are not good rulers. They are men who have led their people in child sacrifice; and who have rejected the path of peace with God's people in favour of an attempt to exterminate them (v 1-4).

> ❷ *What does Joshua do with their bodies (v 26)?*

> ❷ *Read Deuteronomy 21:22-23. What is Joshua saying about these kings?*

> ❷ *Read Galatians 3:13-14. What happened to God's King, the Christ? Why did he do this?*

By nature, we line up with Adoni-Zedek; not born into Israel, and living as enemies of God. Our actions may be different to his; our natural attitude is the same. We deserve to be cursed; and the only reason we are not facing the death these five kings did is because another King was cursed in our place, hanging on a tree until he died so that we might enjoy life as members of God's people, instead of judgment outside them.

⌃ Pray

Thank the Lord Jesus that he won his ultimate victory in weakness, hanging on a tree, under a curse… for you. Ask him to give you the privilege of being part of the way he works to triumph in his world.

Bible in a year: Exodus 9 – 12

Taking the land

This is a long section about the ongoing conquest of the land by Joshua. We'll take a whistlestop tour, pausing to notice a few of the highlights.

Why Joshua won

Read Joshua 10:28-43

The headline is simple: Joshua won.

❓ *But why did he win (v 42)?*

Imagine you're an Israelite living centuries later, reading this record of your ancestors' crushing victories.

❓ *Why would you need to remember v 42?*

···· TIME OUT ··

❓ *When we read of great revivals and spiritual victories of the church in ages past, why do we need to remember v 42?*

❓ *Why would we need to remember it if revival came to our church today?*

Who Joshua beat

Read Joshua 11:1-11

❓ *How is the superiority of Israel's enemies underlined here?*

The point is: this is like the Belize national guard taking on the US army!

❓ *What does God promise Joshua (v 6)? How does Joshua respond (v 7)?*

Once again, Israel defeats this great alliance of northern city-kings (v 7-11). Notice that trusting in God doesn't mean becoming passive as we wait for promises to be fulfilled. God promised victory: so Joshua fought. God's promises prompt confident action.

⌄ Apply

God has promised that the nations will hear about his Son (Acts 1:8).

❓ *Are you waiting for that to happen, or working to be part of the way that happens? How?*

God has promised that he will make you like his Son (Romans 8:29).

❓ *Are you waiting for him to do that, or working to become that person? How?*

How Joshua led

Read Joshua 11:12-23

❓ *How does the writer sum up Joshua's leadership (v 15)?*

Joshua is the great example of a man who led God's people to live God's way.

If you have time, **read 12:1 – 13:33.** It seems merely a list of defeated kings and occupied towns; but the subtext on every line is: God keeps his promises. Each victory is his gift; each town his blessing.

⌃ Pray

Pray for the national and local leaders of your church. Pray that they would be no less than Joshua, leading you to obey God; and that they would be no more than Joshua, seeking not to change God's laws but to submit to them.

 Bible in a year: 1 Samuel 26 – 31

An action man of faith

Decades before, Joshua and eleven other Israelites had spied out the promised land. Ten had advised against invasion, since the inhabitants were so strong.

Joshua and one other had advised invasion, since God was even stronger (Numbers 14:6-9). That one other was a man named Caleb. He and Joshua were the only two from those twelve to enter the promised land.

The bigger they are…

Read Joshua 14:1-15

❷ *What has God done for Caleb already (v 9-11)?*

❷ *What does Caleb now want to do (v 12)?*

The Anakites were huge. The spies who had explored the land decades before had said that compared to the Anakites "we seemed like grasshoppers in our own eyes, and we looked the same to them" (Numbers 13:33). And the most intimidating of them lived in Hebron (Joshua 14:15).

❷ *So how does Caleb's request in verse 12 display his complete trust in God?*

… the harder they fall

Read Joshua 15:1-15

❷ *How do we see God keeping his promises here?*

❷ *How do we see Caleb trusting God here?*

Again, God's promises to his people are kept as his people courageously act in line with them. Why does Caleb gain his inheritance? Both because God had promised to give it to him, and because he went in and took it.

☑ Apply

"You do not have, because you do not ask God" (James 4:2).

❷ *Are there things you don't ask God for because you don't really think he can, or will, give them to you?*

❷ *Are there ways you hold back from taking risks to obey God because you don't really trust he'll give you what you need?*

From the safe distance of 3,000 years, I applaud what Caleb did; then I find it far harder when courageous trust is called for in my own life!

❷ *How will remembering God's promises help us next time we're called to trust him as we obey him?*

The next generation

Read Joshua 15:16-19

❷ *How are Othniel and Aksah similar to Caleb?*

Caleb's confidence in God's promises rubs off on those around him.

☑ Apply

❷ *How can you encourage others to live by faith in God's promises?*

❷ *Do you know any radically obedient Christians, whose example it would be good to follow?*

Seeds of disaster

Not all Israel followed Caleb's example. Today we see seeds of trouble, and hints of what prevents God's people from enjoying his blessing..

Disobedient compromise

Skim-read Joshua 15:20-63

❓ *How successfully does Judah occupy their inheritance (note v 63)?*

But failing to dislodge the Jebusites doesn't seem like a big deal, particularly when it follows a long list of occupation.

Read Exodus 23:32-33

❓ *What's the problem with Judah's compromise?*

Read Joshua 16:10; 17:11-13 (or if you have time, 16:1 – 17:13)

❓ *How do the tribes of Ephraim and Manasseh treat the Canaanites?*

The book of Judges will tell of an Israel which loses all God's blessings. Why? Because they keep worshipping the gods of those who live among them (Judges 2:11). And why are those people there? Because Israel "did not dislodge" them. Compromise turned into catastrophe.

❤ Apply

❓ *Take an honest look at your life. Where are you, or where are you in danger of, settling for nearly-but-not-quite-fully obeying God?*

❓ *What would uncompromising obedience in that area of your life look like?*

Discontented distrust

Read Joshua 17:14-18

❓ *Why are the tribes of Joseph's sons (Manasseh and Ephraim) not content (v 14, 16)?*

Remember, Caleb had simply gone and taken the land God had promised him.

❓ *Why won't the Joseph tribes do the same (v 16)?*

❓ *How does Joshua challenge them (v 17)?*

⬆ Pray

❓ *What are the circumstances you wish God had ordered differently?*

Why not thank him for those specific circumstances now, and ask him to show you how you can use them to obey him. Ask him to help you guard against discontentment.

Delaying in inactivity

Read Joshua 18:1-10 (or 18:1 – 19:51)

❓ *What has God given these seven tribes (18:3)?*

❓ *So why don't they yet live there?!*

Tomorrow always sounds like a great day to make that lifestyle change, to stop that sin, to obey God more radically. We need to hear Joshua's challenge: how long will we wait? Will we get on with living for God today?

❤ *Bible in a year: Job 31 – 32*

Not just any old town

In Israel, there were two types of special towns. Both are a picture of how God's people live under God's rule and blessing.

Cities of refuge

Read Joshua 20:1-9

❷ *If someone committed manslaughter, what could they do? How would this protect them?*

I recently heard of an Albanian pastor who was killed as part of a blood feud between two families that has continued for generations. His young son is now being pressurised to avenge his father's death. And so the cycle continues…

❷ *How did cities of refuge break that cycle in Israel?*

These verses underline the value God places on human life. God cares that the unintentional killer is not caught up in a blood feud. But he also cares that there was a death at all, however accidental. The killer may be safe in a city of refuge; but he cannot leave it and return to his old life even if he is found not guilty of murder at trial. The city of refuge is both a place of safety and a prison. It's life but not real life.

❷ *Until when (v 6)?*

Is this a glimmer of the gospel? Only the high priest's death can release a man from the consequences of his actions, so that he can freely enjoy life in God's land. And the ultimate High Priest is Jesus, whose death frees us to live with God eternally.

⌃ Pray

Thank God that he cares about us. Ask him to enable you to reflect that care in your attitudes and actions. Thank God that his Son is your High Priest, whose death releases you from a life without freedom or blessing.

Towns for Levites

Read Joshua 21:1-42

The Levites were the tribe of Israel set apart to act as priests. This involved both bringing Israel's sacrifices to God, and teaching Israel about God. (See Deuteronomy 33:10.)

❷ *Why was it vital that all Israelites had a Levite living nearby?*

The Levites received a place to live and a way to provide for themselves (Joshua 21:2-3), taken from the inheritance of the rest of Israel. We don't have Levite priests today; but we do have those who are set apart to point us to Jesus' ultimate sacrifice, and to teach us how to live for God. We need them to be near us; and we need to provide for them from what the Lord has given us.

⌃ Pray

Thank God for your church's pastor(s). Ask God to enable them to keep pointing you to Christ, and teaching you God's ways. Ask him to show you how you can support your pastor and his family, materially as well as in prayer.

Bible in a year: Jeremiah 17 – 21

Civil war averted

Joshua closes with three "summonings" (22:1-34; 23:1-2; 24:1). But before Joshua begins his summons, the writer sums up the book as a whole.

Every one fulfilled

Read Joshua 21:43-45

❷ *What has God given his people?*

❷ *How is verse 45 a good summary of the main teaching of the whole of the book of Joshua?*

⌃ Pray

We have a God who keeps his promises. Always. Without fail. Thank him for this now.

East in west

Read Joshua 22:1-9

The men Joshua summons are those who lived east of the Jordan, but who had fought to win their fellow Israelites their inheritance west of the Jordan, as Joshua had asked (1:12-18).

❷ *How does Joshua describe them (22:2-3)?*

❷ *What should they now do (v 5)?*

Again, we see the combination of praise of God for what he has done (v 4) with encouragement of God's people for the part they have played (v 3). The 16th-century commentator, Matthew Henry, put it like this: "God must be chiefly eyed in our praises, yet instruments must not altogether be overlooked". Or as a friend of mine puts it, "Praise God, and pat the donkey!"

East vs west

Read Joshua 22:10-20

❷ *How do the western tribes react to the eastern Israelites building their altar (v 11-14)?*

❷ *Why? What is their concern (v 16-18)?*

God had been very clear that there was only to be one altar for offering sacrifices to him (Deuteronomy 12:1-6, 13-14).

From a western perspective, this new altar looks like deliberate disobedience to the Lord. And they will not stand idly by!

East meets west

Read Joshua 22:21-34

❷ *How do the eastern tribes reply to the accusation (v 22-28)?*

Far from being an attempt to become independent from God and his people, the altar is intended to keep the eastern tribes' descendants in godly unity with the westerners. War is averted (v 33).

⌄ Apply

❷ *How much do you care about the faith of the generation growing up after you? How does (or should) this influence your prayers and words?*

 Bible in a year: Mark 11 – 12

My God is bigger

I once had a rugby teammate named Wuzza. He was enormous. No matter how intimidating the opposition, if they had no one Wuzza's size, I wasn't worried.

This psalm reminds us that when we trust in God, we trust in someone bigger than any problem we could face.

Out of the frying pan

Read 1 Samuel 21:10-15

David has fled Israel, where King Saul wants him dead, and sought refuge in Gath. Given that Gath's most famous son was Goliath (17:4), it's not surprising that things don't turn out so well when the inhabitants realise who David is. If you have time, turn to Psalm 34 to see how David praised God when he escaped...

On the run

Read Psalm 56:1-7

❷ *What are the different dangers that David is facing in these verses?*

❷ *Can you think of ways that these verses are fulfilled in the life of Jesus?*

God sees, knows, cares

Read Psalm 56:8-13

God may be running a universe, but verse 8 shows that he cares intimately for each one of us. No child of God ever shed an unseen tear.

It's important to remember David's encounter with Goliath some years earlier. The Israelite soldiers were all quaking in their

sandals because Goliath was literally twice the size of them. But David made a different comparison. He did not compare himself to the giant but the giant to God: "Who is this uncircumcised Philistine that he should defy the armies of the living God?" (1 Samuel 17:26). Now in Goliath's home town, David fights fear the same way.

❷ *What comparison does he make in Psalm 56:4 and 10-11?*

❷ *How confident is David that God will do as he has promised and deliver him?*

⌄ Apply

❷ *When are you tempted to give in to fear of man, rather than to trust in God?*

❷ *What problems or anxieties are you facing at the moment?*

❷ *What determines whether you feel confident and calm to face them, or overwhelmed and sleepless with anxiety?*

⌃ Pray

Take time to think about where in the Bible you see God deal with situations like that.

Now pray for the things that worry you and for those you love, in the light of verses 4 and 10-11.

Bible in a year: 2 Corinthians 1 – 3

You have been warned

By chapter 23, Joshua is a very old man. These last two chapters are his final words to the people of God...

You have seen...

Read Joshua 23:1-5

❷ *What have these key leaders in Israel "seen"?*

❷ *What will they "see" (v 5)?*

Why? Because "the LORD your God promised you" that this would happen.

···· TIME OUT ·····································

Joshua's logic is: you saw God's grace to you yesterday, so you can trust God's grace to you today and tomorrow. You can live in confident, joyful obedience, trusting him to give you all you need.

Read Romans 8:31-32

We can look back and see Jesus dying on a cross for us. How can we doubt that God will give us anything and everything else we need to enjoy a life of blessing?

❷ *How does this help you to give things up to obey God?*

❷ *How does this help you when God withholds something you thought would make your life better (money, relationships, promotion, etc.)?*

Be careful

Read Joshua 23:6-11

❷ *What positive things should Israel do (v 6, 8, 11)?*

❷ *What will this mean not doing (v 7)?*

❷ *How does verse 9 remind Israel of the foolishness of turning away from God in order to love and serve the gods of other nations?*

Why should Israel obey the Lord and avoid other "gods"? Because the true God "fights for you, just as he promised".

But if...

Read Joshua 23:12-16

❷ *What does God promise about his response to...*
  • *disobedient compromise (v 12-13)?*
  • *covenant unfaithfulness (v 15-16)?*

Verse 7 shows us who faces God's promised judgment. It is not the person who sins, repents, and seeks forgiveness. It is the person who consistently and unapologetically serves and loves other gods.

❷ *How do we know God will judge?*

Because "every promise has been fulfilled" (v 14). The truth that God always keeps his promises is a wonderful encouragement; it is also a warning, to us today as to the people back then.

⌄ Apply

Notice that verse 16 finishes with a challenge.

❷ *How do you need to hear Joshua's warning as you finish this study today?*

Happy ending, with a twist

Now Joshua summons the whole of Israel one last time. They meet at the place where centuries before God had promised to give Abraham this land (Genesis 12:7).

The Lord

Read Joshua 24:1-13

Here is God's history lesson. And the main player throughout is God himself. History truly is his story.

❷ *Focus on the "gave" actions of God. What has God given his people (v 3, 4, 8, 11, 13)?*

❷ *How is verse 13 a good summary of the period of history covered in the book of Joshua?*

The choice

Read Joshua 24:14-18

❷ *What is the choice that confronts the people of Israel (v 14-15)?*

Then, as now, there was a great range of gods, ideas and philosophies to trust in, to look to, to worship. But then, as now, there was really only one choice: serve the God of the Bible or serve something else as your god.

❷ *What do the people choose? Why (v 16-18)?*

If the book of Joshua ended here, it would be a wonderfully upbeat ending to a book of triumph and blessing. But Joshua has something devastating to say...

The problem

Read Joshua 24:19-27

❷ *What does Joshua warn the people (v 19-20)?*

❷ *How do they respond (v 21, 24)?*

The book ends with this debate unresolved. Who's right? Are God's people capable of continued obedience to him (as they insist), or will they turn aside from his blessings (as Joshua claims)?

Tragically, the rest of the Old Testament is one long argument in favour of Joshua's view. There is simply something wrong with the human heart. Even when we have seen God's work in the world and in our own lives; even when we commit to obeying him as our God; we find ourselves unable to love and serve him as we should. Despite all his goodness to us, we call disaster upon ourselves (v 20).

Read John 3:16-18

❷ *What has God given (v 16)? Why is this great news for people like us, who deserve disaster?*

Read Ezekiel 11:19-20

❷ *Why is what God gives here great news for people like us, who aren't able to obey him?*

◤ Pray

Thank God for all he has done in human history. Thank him for all he has done for you. Thank him that he has given you a perfect future in his perfect land, obeying him perfectly as you enjoy all his blessings.

Bible in a year: 2 Samuel 1 – 4

The end of Joshua

The end of Joshua reads like a set of directions to some graves! But this is not a mere obituary...

Joshua and Eleazar

Read Joshua 24:28-31, 33

❓ Why might what happens in verse 28 have seemed very unlikely at the beginning of the book of Joshua?

❓ Where is Joshua buried (v 30)?

You could tell the history of God's people by using burial sites. The baby boys killed in Egypt (Exodus 1:22)... the disobedient Israelites in the desert (Numbers 14:26-30)... Moses on the edge of the land (Deuteronomy 34:5-8)... Joshua, and his high priest, Eleazar, in the land of their inheritance.

Joseph

Read Genesis 50:24-26

At this point, Joseph is prime minister of Egypt. His life has been a story of riches to rags to riches. But he dies wealthy, surrounded by his family, at peace.

❓ So what is remarkable about what he says his family need God to do in verse 25?

❓ How do his instructions about his bones display his faith in God's promises?

◣ Apply

❓ Are you more interested and excited by what this world offers you, or by what you'll have in the land God has promised to bring his people into?

Read Joshua 24:32

❓ What is hugely significant about where Joseph's bones are laid to rest?

Death is the end

Joshua was a courageous, obedient leader. But this book ends with his death, just as Genesis ends with Joseph's death, and Deuteronomy with Moses'. God's people may enjoy God's blessings in God's land—but the gravestones are a cold reminder that it cannot be for ever.

We must wait until the New Testament to find Bible books that end not with a body in a grave but with a tomb that is empty. It's in the resurrection of the Lord Jesus that we discover the way into "an inheritance that can never perish, spoil, or fade ... kept in heaven for you" (1 Peter 1:4). As God's people, we can obey him courageously as we travel there, because he has promised to get us there. And God always keeps his promises...

◣ Pray

Thank the Lord Jesus for the inheritance he has won for you, and given you, and is bringing you to.

◣ Apply

❓ How has the book of Joshua encouraged you to trust God more deeply and obey God more fully?

ACTS: A hard ask

We are back in Acts. Jesus has just called Saul on the road to Damascus. Next, he wants to bring another believer alongside him. But the other believer is not so sure…

Obeying Jesus

Read Acts 9:7-9

It's unclear whether Saul's companions heard the specifics of what Jesus said or something more general, like a loud boom. The word translated "sound" (v 7) could refer to either. What is clear is that Saul heard the voice. He knew what he needed to do.

❷ Look back at verse 6—what had Jesus commanded Saul to do?

❷ What did Saul do (v 8)?

---- TIME OUT ----

❷ Why do you think the Lord blinded Saul for three days? What emotions would sudden blindness create in you?

Hearing Jesus

Read Acts 9:10-16

Jesus gave specific instructions to Ananias (v 11). Like Moses in Exodus 3 – 4, however, Ananias hesitated to obey.

❷ What reasons did Ananias give for his hesitancy (Acts 9:13-14)?

❷ Were those reasons valid, do you think?

❷ For what purposes did Jesus choose Saul (v 15-16)?

❤ Apply

Ananias accurately depicted Saul's terror

campaign. Yet still the Lord told him to go to him (v 15).

❷ When was the last time the Spirit prompted you to do something but you hesitated, based on a number of valid reasons?

❷ Is there anything hard he is calling you to today? Will you trust him, and obey?

❤ Pray

Saul's ministry of proclamation and suffering paved the way for the good news about Jesus to spread throughout the Roman world. Pray for missionaries who carry the message of Jesus that the Holy Spirit would bear fruit through them. Lift any you know by name before the Lord now.

Obeying Jesus

Read Acts 9:17-19

❷ How did Ananias address Saul (v 17)? Why is this significant?

❷ Though the phrase "signs and wonders" does not appear, what miracle accompanied Saul's conversion (v 18)?

❤ Apply

❷ What people has God given you to journey with? What can you do this week to support one another as followers of Jesus?

Bible in a year: Job 33 – 34

Fearless for Jesus

Saul came to Damascus to imprison followers of Jesus and take them back to Jerusalem. But God had other plans!

Baffled opponents

Read Acts 9:19-22

❓ What two things did Saul do in Damascus (v 19-20)?

❓ Who did Saul say Jesus is (v 20, 22)?

❓ What did the Jews in Damascus know about Saul (v 21)?

You've likely heard stories of people whose lives God completely upended—drug dealers turned pastors, atheists turned evangelists, star athletes turned vocal witnesses. Saul was very much in that category of "totally unexpected but totally amazing" conversions!

Read Acts 9:23-25

❓ What implicit role did the church play in Saul's development (v 22)?

❓ What explicit role did the church play in Saul's escape (v 25)?

⌄ Apply

Perhaps your conversion was dramatic. But maybe you've believed in Jesus for as long as you can remember. Same with me. We may wish we had a more shocking story. But you are no less a testimony of God's power and grace. All of us are sinners. All of us needed saving. Pause to praise God now for the way he worked in your life, whether it was before you can remember or in a spectacular and memorable way.

❓ What parts of your story highlight God's mercy to you? What are some ways you can share your story with others?

Baffled believers

The Jews in Damascus weren't the only ones baffled by Saul's transformation!

Read Acts 9:26

❓ What emotion did the disciples experience (v 26)?

❓ What false belief gave rise to this feeling (v 26)?

False beliefs always generate fear. We feel it in our bodies. Noticing our physical response can be a great tool to combat false belief. When we feel fear in our body, we can ask ourselves, "What false belief is driving this fear?" Then we can speak the gospel to ourselves: "I belong to my faithful Saviour, Jesus Christ. The Lord is the one shepherding me, so I lack nothing. I am the beloved child of God."

Read Acts 9:27-31

Barnabas's intervention opened the door not only for the church to enjoy fellowship with Saul but for the gospel to advance in Jerusalem, and eventually Caesarea and Tarsus.

⌄ Apply

❓ Who is on the margins of your church? How can you bring them further in?

 Bible in a year: Jeremiah 22 – 26

A second wave

In Acts 1 – 5 Peter is central to the story, but since then Luke has mostly focused on others. Now Peter is back front and centre—with explosive growth following him.

Awakening in Lydda

Read Acts 9:31

After Stephen's martyrdom set off a terrifying period of persecution, this verse reports "a time of peace".

❓ *How does Luke describe this season?*

Persecution had scattered believers everywhere, preaching the word and making disciples wherever they went (8:4). The report of conversions in Samaria then prompted Peter and John to take a trip to confirm that this really was a work of the Spirit (8:14-17). Now with a pause in persecution Peter took the chance to check on churches elsewhere.

Read Acts 9:32-35

❓ *What was the result of Peter's healing in the name of Jesus (v 35)?*

Citywide movements of God are often called awakenings, since people awaken en masse to the good news about Jesus.

❓ *How might your city or town be different if "all those who live[d]" there "turned to the Lord" (v 35)?*

Awakening in Joppa

Read Acts 9:36-39

Throughout the Bible God expresses his affection for the widow, the orphan, the immigrant, and the poor: four groups that the ancient world frequently ostracised.

⌄ Apply

❓ *Who do you know in these categories? How can you show God's love to them this week?*

Strengthening and growing

Read Acts 9:40-43

Note how Peter's visits differ from Saul's (Paul's) later missionary journeys. Paul made it his "ambition to preach the gospel where Christ was not known" (Romans 15:20). Today we call that "church planting"—Paul started churches. But Peter didn't travel to start churches. He went to check on already existing churches, to make sure they were well.

One thing was the same, though. Wherever they went, large numbers of people turned to Jesus. You might say that those who start churches are part of a "first wave" of evangelism, while Peter's work of strengthening the churches brought about a "second wave", adding new believers to the churches already there.

⌄ Apply

❓ *What has this passage taught you to aim for, and pray for, when it comes to your own church?*

A cave with a view

There's something about suffering and discouragement that makes the world close in on us. We can retreat into a cave, and struggle to see anything but our own difficulties.

Psalm 57 finds David in that situation. What's more, he's literally in a cave too. But his cave has a view...

The bird and the beasts

Read Psalm 57:1-5

❷ *David was a mighty warrior, but what does he long to do in verse 1?*

❷ *Why is he so desperate, according to verses 3-4?*

As a shepherd he fought lions and bears (1 Samuel 17:34-36). He sees his enemies now as like wild animals. Weary of running and fighting and hiding, he longs to curl up safely like a chick under its mother's wings. But even from the depths of a dark, dank cave, he sees God exalted over the heavens (Psalm 57:5).

Poetic justice

Read Psalm 57:6-11

❷ *Why is the fate of the wicked in verse 6 so fitting and just?*

Verses 7-10 make for a bizarre image: David and his friends are meant to be hiding quietly in a cave, but David is blasting out music and singing at the top of his voice!

❷ *What is it that causes him to wake up his friends with singing (v 10)?*

The second half of the psalm finishes with the same words as the first half (v 11, 5):

David knows that the good news of the true God should be shared with all people across the world (v 9), and that God's love and faithfulness reach up beyond outer space (v 10).

⌄ Apply

At the heart of this psalm we find David stuck in a cave and yet able to see God exalted above the heavens, and worshipped all around the world. He cannot see these things with his eyes, but he has God's promises and that is enough for him. What about us? Am I ever able to praise God before he has rescued me? Am I ever able to see by faith that one day we will live for ever in a place of laughter and delight? This sort of faith is blind, but it is not stupid. It is built upon the faithfulness of God. The Bible is full of promises made and promises kept—in particular the central promise of God coming to us to save us. That promise was fulfilled in the life, death and resurrection of Jesus (2 Corinthians 1:20). When God has done that, surely we can trust him for the things we can't yet see!

⌃ Pray

Pray the words of verse 11. Pray that God would enable you to keep praying that prayer even when you feel lonely and beleaguered as a Christian; even when you can't see any evidence of God's power and love for you; and even when the gospel appears to be making no progress in your particular "cave".

The centurion's vision

Luke shifts our attention from Joppa to Caesarea, 30 miles up the Mediterranean coast. There we find someone begging God to act.

God's answer changed everything—for him and for the church!

The man

Read Acts 10:1-2

Caesarea was built by Herod the Great. The Roman governor kept a home there, which necessitated a strong presence of the Roman army. Cornelius was a "centurion" in that army, a commander of 100 troops.

But there's more to Cornelius.

❓ *What adjectives does Luke use to describe Cornelius (v 2)?*

❓ *What good works were associated with him?*

A "God-fearing" person describes a Gentile who converted to Judaism and followed the law of Moses. Cornelius was not your typical centurion in the Roman army!

The vision

Read Acts 10:3-4

❓ *What did Cornelius see?*

❓ *What did he hear?*

❓ *How did he feel?*

Luke goes on to repeat that Cornelius's vision occurred "at about three in the afternoon" (v 3).

❓ *Read Acts 3:1. Why was this time of day important to Jews? What does this say about Cornelius's devotion to the Lord?*

❓ *Read Luke 23:44-46. Why was this time of day important to the early church?*

The word "prayed" in Acts 10:2 indicates a kind of pleading or begging. Cornelius wasn't just going through the motions; he longed for God to do something. The phrase "memorial offering" (Acts 10:4) suggests Cornelius longed for God to fulfil his promises to the Jews, and begged God to include him in their fulfilment.

The instructions

Read Acts 10:5-8

❓ *Why had Peter gone to Joppa in the first place? (See Acts 9:38-39 if you don't remember.)*

⌃ Pray

In every single circumstance God accomplishes thousands of purposes. We may ask why God does what he does, but we can be confident that he has us where he wants us—and he has good purposes for us and for others in planting us where we are.

Offer a prayer of surrender to God for where he has you right now. Acknowledge his lordship over your life, and ask him for the grace to be content with and fruitful in your current circumstances.

The apostle's vision

Luke shifts our attention to Joppa where a second vision is about to complement the one we read about yesterday.

The trance

Read Acts 10:9-12

Verse 3 says that Cornelius had a "vision". So what's the difference between a vision and a trance? Not much, actually. A "vision" describes what the person saw, while a "trance" focuses on the person's state of amazement while having a vision.

···· TIME OUT ····

Read Deuteronomy 14:3-21

What four-legged animals did Moses prohibit the Israelites from eating? What about birds? Reptiles? (See Leviticus 11:29-31.)

❷ *According to Deuteronomy 14:2 and 14:21, what was the reason for the prohibition?*

The primary meaning of holiness is not super spirituality. It means to be special, set apart for a unique purpose—like fine china or a Formula One racecar. God calls us to live differently (1 Peter 1:15-16) because he himself is the unique one (Isaiah 40:25-26). There is no one like him!

The dialogue

Read Acts 10:13-16

It's hard to appreciate fully Peter's cognitive dissonance here. The voice told him one thing, but the Old Testament seemed to have told him another. And he was determined to be faithful to God and his word.

 Bible in a year: 2 Samuel 5 – 9

···· TIME OUT ····

❷ *In what ways does this scenario resemble Jesus' temptation in the wilderness (Luke 4:1-4)? How do we know that Peter didn't think Satan was talking to him (Acts 10:14)?*

❷ *What lesson did God want Peter to learn from this vision (v 15)?*

The convergence

Read Acts 10:17-23

❷ *According to v 20, who sent the three men? According to v 8, who sent them? What does this teach us about the Spirit?*

Contrary to custom (see v 28) Peter invited these Gentiles into the house. Inviting them in seemed to contradict literally the call to be holy, to be set apart from the rest.

▲ Pray

The Holy One came to live with us (John 1:14), not only to bring us into God's house but to make us God's house (Hebrews 3:6)! Give thanks to God for the earth-shattering, boundary-destroying work of Jesus!

▼ Apply

❷ *God challenged Peter to reconsider what it means to be holy. In light of the gospel, what sets you apart? Hint: the answer is not what you do!*

Here to listen

It's easy to think this story is only about Peter and Cornelius. The headings in your Bible—and of our last two studies!—put them at the centre.

But the gospel always creates community. And today's passage shines a light on those who are gathered around the two main characters.

The others

Read Acts 10:23-24

❷ *Who accompanied Peter (v 23)? Why do you think they went along?*

One reason Luke includes this detail is to introduce multiple witnesses to this historic event. In both Acts 11 and Acts 15, what happened at Cornelius's house would inspire and ultimately resolve controversy. By sending other believers with him, God ensured Peter would not be the sole witness to his surprising work.

❷ *Who was with Cornelius (Acts 10:24)? Why do you think he invited them to hear Peter?*

Apply

Sharing Jesus with family and friends can be difficult. It's hard to know what to say and when and how to say it. One simple approach is to invite them to worship with you. As they hear the gospel expressed in song, Scripture, and sermon, you'll have opportunities to chat about your faith.

❷ *Who could you simply invite to join you at your church this weekend?*

The reception

Read Acts 10:25-29

❷ *What posture did Cornelius take before Peter? What does this tell you about Cornelius's heart?*

❷ *How did Peter respond to Cornelius's posture? What does this tell you about Peter's heart?*

❷ *What did Peter say was the lesson of his vision (v 28)?*

Pray

❷ *Is there any "type" of person you are likely to see as "impure or unclean"—too far from Jesus to respond, or too unworthy to seek to reach with the gospel?*

This may include groups of people or specific individuals. Confess your sin of partiality to the Lord, and ask him to renew your heart with the love of Jesus for those you deem unworthy.

The purpose

Read Acts 10:30-33

❷ *What is Cornelius's attitude to what Peter is about to say?*

Pray that the same would be true of you—that as you open the pages of the New Testament, you would have a sense of expectancy, eager to hear Christ's apostles speak to you.

The good news of peace

Today we come to Peter's message to Cornelius—one we need to hear every day!

I now realise

Read Acts 10:34-35

We could (mis)read verse 35 as teaching salvation by good works: *God will accept you if you fear him and do what is right.* Yet the Scriptures are clear. No one fears God and does what is right. (See Romans 3:10-12.)

What, then, is Acts 10:35 talking about? Wait and see!

Life of Jesus

Read Acts 10:36-38

When we present the gospel, we often skip from the incarnation to the crucifixion, from Jesus' birth to his death. But the apostles lay stress on his life.

- ❷ *What did God announce through Jesus (v 36)?*
- ❷ *What did God do for Jesus (v 38)?*
- ❷ *Peter emphasises two activities from Jesus' life (v 38). What are they?*
- ❷ *How was Jesus able to do these things (v 38)?*

"The one who fears [God] and does what is right" (v 35) is none other than Jesus! The good news is that God accepts the one who always feared him and did what was right— Jesus. And since the Spirit has made us one with Jesus, God accepts us in him. That's why it doesn't matter what nation we're from. Divine acceptance comes not from our family of origin but from our connection to Jesus.

◢ Pray

This is why we pray in Jesus' name—because we are "accepted in the beloved" (Ephesians 1:6, KJV). Give thanks for your sure standing in Jesus, for his acceptance of you because you are one with him.

Death and resurrection

Read Acts 10:39-43

Note how often Peter underscored the "witnesses".

- ❷ *Why was this such an important part of his message, do you think?*
- ❷ *What proof did Peter give that Jesus physically came back from the dead (v 40-41)?*
- ❷ *What did Jesus command his witnesses to do (v 42)?*
- ❷ *What promise did Peter hold out to his audience (v 43)?*

◢ Pray

Confess your faith in Jesus again. Acknowledge him to be the "Lord of all" (v 36) and the "judge of the living and the dead" (v 42). Thank him for the forgiveness of all your sins, which is for his glory and your good.

The surprising Spirit

"You hear [the wind's] sound, but you cannot tell where it comes from or where it is going," Jesus said. "So it is with everyone born of the Spirit" (John 3:8).

In today's passage the Spirit goes somewhere the believers do not expect!

The Spirit's outpouring

Read Acts 10:44-46

❷ *How did the "circumcised believers" respond to this movement of the Spirit (v 45)? What was it about the Spirit's outpouring that brought about this reaction (v 45)?*

Like the wind, the Spirit is invisible and yet perceptible.

❷ *What two pieces of evidence proved to the Jewish believers that the Spirit had come upon the Gentiles (v 46)?*

⌄ Apply

Christians hold widely divergent views on the work of the Holy Spirit. But all of us would do well to remember that we cannot restrict or control the Wind. He moves where and how he chooses, and that may well sometimes be contrary to what we expect. If nothing else, we should expect at times to be astonished by how and where God's Spirit moves—an expectation that might cultivate a little humility within each of us. And that would be good for all of us!

❷ *Do you live with this kind of expectation? Why/why not?*

Peter's conclusion

Read Acts 10:47-48

❷ *On what basis did Peter conclude that Cornelius and his guests should be baptised (v 47)?*

There's a subtle shift in Peter's language in these verses. In verse 47 he foresaw potential opposition and concluded, "Surely no one can stand in the way of their being baptised with water". But then Luke says in verse 48 that Peter "ordered" that they undergo Christian baptism.

❷ *Why was it important that Cornelius and his guests were baptised at the explicit instruction of Peter? (Hint: consider the potential opposition that Peter foresaw.)*

⌃ Pray

Praise God for the surprising work of his Spirit in your life. Ask him to bear his fruit in and through you, so that you might be an instrument to turn others towards Jesus.

Bible in a year: Jeremiah 27 –31

Objections

The surprising work of God's Spirit doesn't always cause only joy. In the case of Cornelius, it brought criticism—from people in the church.

Read Acts 11:1-3

❷ *What had the believers in Judea heard about the Gentiles (v 1)?*

❷ *What was the point of contention for the Jewish believers (v 3)?*

In response Peter told them what Jesus had revealed to him.

What the Lord had shown

Read Acts 11:4-10

There isn't an Old Testament law forbidding the Israelites from eating with Gentiles. The prohibition arose from tradition as a way to mark how pure someone was. But unlike this custom, the Hebrew Bible clearly stipulated what Jews may and may not *eat*. What Peter saw (v 6) was a hoard of unclean animals.

❷ *Imagine you are one of the Jewish believers critical of Peter's conduct. At this point in his story, what do you imagine your response would have been?*

❷ *What lesson did God want Peter—and by extension other Jewish believers—to learn from the vision (v 9)?*

What the Lord had arranged

Read Acts 11:11-14

❷ *Look back at the criticism of Peter in v 3. Did he dispute their charge (v 12)?*

❷ *Who did Peter say gave him authority to ignore Jewish tradition (v 12)?*

What the Lord had said

Read Acts 11:15-18

❷ *How had Jesus prepared Peter for the moment of Cornelius's conversion (v 16)? What word had the Lord given him?*

Note the phrase "at the beginning" in verse 15.

❷ *To what event was Peter referring? (Hint: see Acts 2:1-4.) What began on that day?*

⚆ Apply

When the unexpected happens, in our astonishment we can turn to God's word to help us interpret what's going on. The diligent work of reading, studying, and meditating on Scripture—what you're doing right now!—is preparing you for what lies ahead. You might not see it now, but your work will reap a harvest.

⚆ Pray

"Even to Gentiles God has granted repentance that leads to life" (Acts 11:18). Give thanks for this truth and what it means for you personally.

 Bible in a year: Mark 15 – 16

The joy of judgment

What happens when people get away with bad behaviour?

The bully who makes life a misery for others at school. The business leader who gets rich running the company into the ground. The husband or wife who is committing adultery and still coming to church.

Unjust judges

Read Psalm 58:1-5

We are used to mocking our politicians. So often we view them as laughable incompetents—material for comedy shows. But there is nothing remotely funny about the behaviour of the rulers in verses 1-5.

❓ *What is going on, and what images does David use to press the message home?*

Joyful judgment

Read Psalm 58:6-11

❓ *What does David call on God to do in verses 6-10?*

These images might make you feel uncomfortable. We need to remember though that David is writing in a more brutal time, and these are just Old Testament ways of saying *this is what it will be like for them to experience true justice for what they have done.*

❓ *What impact does it have when justice is done?*

Verse 11 shows that, ultimately, David is concerned with something even more important than justice being done on earth.

❓ *What happens when people see that God works justice for his people?*

···· TIME OUT ····································

In 1 Timothy 2:1-4 Paul urges us to pray for our leaders. It's not because he cares about politics more than spiritual matters but because politics affects how freely Christians can proclaim and live out the gospel: "I urge, then, first of all, that petitions, prayers, intercession and thanksgiving be made for all people—for kings and all those in authority, that we may live peaceful and quiet lives in all godliness and holiness. This is good, and pleases God our Saviour, who wants all people to be saved and to come to a knowledge of the truth."

▲ Pray

Pray for our leaders and police and judges.

Pray that they would work for justice for all, so that society is fair, and so that people might see daily reminders of the fact that all of us will one day stand before the just God, who rewards goodness and punishes wickedness.

Bible in a year: 2 Corinthians 6 – 8

Belonging to Christ

Now Luke introduces us to five new places, each one further from Jerusalem than the last. Like a pebble thrown into a pond, the message of Jesus is rippling out.

Phoenicia describes a region along the Mediterranean coast north of Galilee. Cyprus is an island in the eastern end of the Mediterranean Sea. Further north is Antioch, an ancient Syrian city but now part of Turkey. Cyrene is an African city in modern-day Libya. And Tarsus, Saul's hometown, is northeast of Antioch, also in modern-day Turkey.

Awakening in Antioch

Read Acts 11:19-21

❓ *What was different about the way the persecuted Christians shared the gospel and the way the people from Cyprus and Cyrene shared the gospel?*

^ Pray

Praise Jesus for his life, his death and his resurrection. Then take out your list of friends and family that you wrote during the Acts studies in the previous issues and pray for them. Ask the Lord's hand to be with you so that they too might believe and turn to Jesus.

Apostolic review

Read Acts 11:22-24

As before (see 8:14-17) the apostles wanted to verify the reports of the gospel spreading in Antioch. So they sent Barnabas to investigate.

❓ *What did we learn about Barnabas in 4:36-37?*

❓ *What else does Luke tell us about Barnabas here in 11:24?*

❓ *When Barnabas saw "what the grace of God had done", what was his emotional response (v 23)?*

❓ *What was his pastoral response (v 23)?*

∨ Apply

Take a moment for self-examination. When you see the grace of God at work, which of these two responses comes more naturally for you? Can you think of someone who more naturally responds the other way? What might you learn from their example?

Finding Saul

Read Acts 11:25-26

As the church grew, the city took notice. That's why residents of Antioch called the believers "Christians", which means "belonging to Christ". They saw that this growing group was something new.

∨ Apply

Look over today's reading and note what the city witnessed in the church.

❓ *How do the people around you see these activities in your church and in your own life?*

Bible in a year: Exodus 21 – 24

Giving as we are able

God employs people and circumstances to bring out the best in us. Today's passage inspires us with a remarkable example of this work of God's Spirit.

A prophet

Read Acts 11:27-28

Prophets appear throughout the Bible. They did not merely predict the future; they also confronted the people for their unfaithfulness to God's law, earning them the ire of leaders both political and religious (7:52). Most significant to Luke, Moses predicted the coming of another prophet who would bring God's word to them (7:37)—fulfilled in none other than Jesus himself (2:30).

But here we find that in the New Testament prophets are part of the church too!

❓ *Read Deuteronomy 18:21-22. How could people determine whether someone truly spoke as a prophet for the Lord?*

❓ *Why do you think Luke added the parenthetical comment at the end of Acts 11:28?*

⏏ Pray

Read Ephesians 4:11-13

❓ *What kinds of leaders does Jesus give his church?*

❓ *Who are the leaders in your community of faith?*

Pray for them by name, that they would "equip his people for works of service, so that the body of Christ may be built up".

A gift

A prophet's words always aim to stir action.

Read Acts 11:29-30

❓ *How did the church at Antioch respond to Agabus's prophecy (v 29)?*

❓ *Look back at Acts 4:32-35. How is their response similar to the early days of the church in Jerusalem?*

The church in Antioch had never met their brothers and sisters in Judea. Nevertheless they gave. This kind of generosity comes from knowing the one who "became poor, so that you through his poverty might become rich" (2 Corinthians 8:9). We give what he has given us and we give in response to how he has given himself to us.

⌄ Apply

For most of us, generosity like this takes planning. It requires holding something in reserve so that, when an unusual need arises, we are able to contribute. It's not just a matter of living on less than you make; it involves earmarking savings for future opportunities to give.

❓ *How might you include this concept into your financial planning?*

❓ *In what ways has this short passage encouraged and/or challenged your current attitude towards giving?*

Bible in a year: 2 Samuel 10 – 14

Persecution and prayer

Now King Herod comes onto the scene. Since there are six different Herods in the New Testament, it's easy to get confused about which is which!

Like the other five, the Herod in today's passage is an evil despot. This Herod is known to historians as Herod Agrippa I. (We'll meet his son, Herod Agrippa II, in Acts 25 – 26, where he's simply called "Agrippa".) The Herod in Acts 12 was the grandson of Herod the Great, the Herod of the Christmas story who killed Bethlehem's children.

James

Read Acts 12:1-2

James is the first apostle to die for his faith, and the only one whose martyrdom is recorded in the New Testament.

James was part of an inner circle among the disciples, together with Peter and his brother John. Luke's Gospel shares some vignettes from James's life. Review these passages to catch a glimpse of him: Luke 5:6-11; 8:51-56; and 9:28-36.

⌃ Pray

Whether we ever face persecution on this scale, we are called to follow Jesus all the days of our lives. So ask God to give you grace to follow him today, and to empower you to "be faithful, even to the point of death" (Revelation 2:10).

Peter

Read Acts 12:3-4

❷ *When was Peter arrested?*

❷ *What did Herod plan to do with him, and when?*

These holy days went all the way back to the exodus. (See Exodus 12.) It was a time appointed to remember God's miraculous deliverance of his people from oppressive slavery in Egypt. But with James martyred and Peter imprisoned, the timing might well have seemed tragically incongruous to the disciples.

The church

Read Acts 12:5

❷ *What is the church's response to the killing of one of its leaders and the arrest of another?*

The Jerusalem church has already seen the power of prayer. (Look back to Acts 4:23-32.) And they are no strangers to persecution (7:54 – 8:3). Times of suffering show what, or who, we truly depend on. We either run towards or away from God—and how quickly we pray, and what we say, is a great revealer of our true spiritual state.

⌃ Pray

❷ *Is there anything that you are facing at the moment in your own strength, rather than in God's? Anything you have stopped praying about, or never started to pray about in the first place?*

Let your answers shape your prayers now.

Bible in a year: Psalm 54 – 56

A way out

When things look hopeless, God delights to make a way.

Unexpected intervention

Read Acts 12:6-7

❓ *What happened once the angel appeared (v 7)?*

❓ *What purpose did each of these things serve?*

Notice that the angel did not appear till the night before the trial. Presumably Peter and the church would have chosen an earlier rescue. But "my thoughts are not your thoughts" the Lord tells us in Isaiah 55:8— and neither is his timing our timing.

⌃ Pray

In what areas of life are you desperate for God to intervene? Take these before the Lord in prayer. Ask him for endurance when you feel like you can't go on.

Vision or reality?

Read Acts 12:8-11

Clearly Herod did not want Peter to escape!

❓ *How many different precautionary measures can you count in these verses?*

In spite of Peter's misunderstanding (v 9), you have to love his inclination to obey. Multiple times the angel told him to do something, and he simply did it. Let's aim

to have the same immediate obedience to God's directives!

Now I know

Read Acts 12:11

❓ *From what two things did the Lord rescue Peter?*

It is a happy ending—kind of. Remember 12:2—the Lord did not do the same thing for James. Perhaps the most challenging aspect of Acts 12 is the opposite fates of these two apostles. This story reminds us that our simplistic assumptions about how God works are woefully inadequate. James's fate reminds us not to assume that God will always intervene in the way we would like, or the way he has done for others. At the same time, Peter's release reminds us not to adopt a stoic approach to life—just grit your teeth and get on with it—or to slide into prayerlessness, as though God can never or would never intervene miraculously.

⌄ Apply

❓ *Are there ways in which you are demanding of God things which he has not promised? What difference will James's story make to you?*

❓ *Are there ways in which you have ceased to ask God things of which he is capable? What difference will Peter's story make to you?*

Bible in a year: Job 37 – 38

I can't believe it

How do we know the Scriptures are true and not just a pious legend? Here's one answer: a story like this would never have made it into a tale of spiritual giants!

Rhoda's joy

Read Acts 12:12-14

❷ *Where did Peter go when he realised he was free (v 12)?*

❷ *Who was there? What were they doing?*

But for now the real story is this hilarious scene. The church was praying for Peter's release, and now he is standing at the door... But out of joy and amazement, Rhoda forgot to let him in!

Details like this authenticate the truthfulness of the Scriptures. Luke is not writing a fictionalised account of what happened. He's telling us what actually occurred, including the all-too-human moments.

⌄ Apply

Stories like this make me wonder how often God has answered a prayer of mine—but I just haven't recognised it.

Read Colossians 4:2

❷ *Think about what you regularly pray about. Have you seen any answers? Might God have already moved to answer your prayer?*

The church's incredulity

Read Acts 12:15-17

❷ *What three responses did the church have to Rhoda's report (v 15-16)?*

Don't miss the humour and humanity of this scene. Rhoda joyfully reports Peter's release—precisely what the church is praying for. But the church can't believe it, and for quite some time Peter remains outside!

Sometimes the church gets it wrong. Sometimes spiritual people get it wrong. Sometimes praying people get it wrong. What marks a person as godly is not that they always get it right. The mark of the godly is humility and a willingness to accept and to change when they get it wrong.

Having introduced us to Mark—the Gospel-writer—in verse 12, in verse 17 Luke mentions James. This isn't James, the brother of John, whom Herod had just put to death. This is James the half-brother of Jesus and the author of the epistle named after him.

⌄ Apply

Let this story cultivate humility in your heart.

❷ *Can you think of ways you've realised you need to change in the last few months? That's good!*

❷ *Are there ways you're being prompted to see you've been getting something wrong (either someone close to you has suggested it, or the Spirit is nudging you)? What will accepting that, and changing, look like?*

❤ *Bible in a year: Jeremiah 32 – 36*

Raised up and struck down

Chapter 12 marks the end of the first part of Acts. The dramatic rescue of Peter might have made a fitting conclusion. But before he finishes part 1, Luke ties up a loose end.

Herod's anger

Read Acts 12:18-19

Given the humour of yesterday's story, one is tempted to chuckle at Luke's understatement in verse 18 ("no small commotion among the soldiers"). But by the end of the paragraph the story has taken a dark and ominous turn.

Herod's approach

Read Acts 12:19-22

❷ *Why did the people of Tyre and Sidon want to reconcile with Herod (v 20)?*

One particularly insidious sin is leveraging what others need in order to get what we want. That's what Herod did here. He took advantage of others' weakness.

But kings are not the only ones guilty of this sin, and it's not always this blatant.

🔽 Apply

❷ *Do you find yourself on either side of this dynamic—the manipulated or the manipulator—in any way?*

❷ *If you are the manipulated, who might help you work through this relationship?*

If you know you are prone to manipulate, ask the Spirit to help you assess honestly the way you treat others.

Herod's demise

Read Acts 12:23-24

The 1st-century Jewish historian Josephus adds to the scene. The people of Tyre and Sidon asked Herod, "Be merciful to us; for although we have hitherto reverenced thee only as a man, yet shall we henceforth own thee as superior to mortal nature". Josephus goes on to say, "The king did neither rebuke them, nor reject their impious flattery".

❷ *Why did God strike Herod down (v 23)?*

❷ *How did God's judgment work itself out (end v 23)?*

❷ *Herod is dead. But what is thriving (v 24)?*

The stark contrast between verse 23 and verse 24 is the pivot from the first part of Acts to the second. Human kings may claim to be God, but eventually succumb to death. God's messengers may be put in prison, but God's word will always "spread and flourish".

🔼 Pray

The essence of our sinful nature is that we put ourselves in the place of God. (See Isaiah 14:14.) Take a moment to acknowledge this waywardness in your own heart and ask God to forgive you because of Jesus. Then praise God that today, as then, his word cannot be chained and his plans cannot be thwarted, even by the most powerful of men.

Wicked words

"Sticks and stones may break my bones, but words will never harm me." We all know the children's rhyme, and most of us have worked out that it's nonsense.

Words have enormous power to cause harm. Think of the child told, "You're useless" or "You're ugly". Think of the celebrity falsely accused of being a paedophile. How do you respond when you're on the receiving end of malicious gossip or cutting words?

We know from the heading of the psalm that the words spoken against David were particularly deadly: his enemies were watching him, ready to tell Saul his movements so Saul could have him attacked when he was vulnerable. (See 1 Samuel 19:11-13.)

There was no **bold** or *italics* option in Hebrew writing. So the writers used structure to stress things. Have a look through and see if you can spot repeated patterns in this psalm.

Read Psalm 59:1-5

❷ *What is David praying for and why?*

Read Psalm 59:11-13

❷ *What does David pray that God will do?*

❷ *What is the impact on others when they see that God is a God of justice?*

Read Psalm 59:6, 14

The ancient Israelites didn't keep dogs as pets. Dogs were vicious, filthy and dangerous, roaming in packs, looking to tear into anything edible they came across.

Read Psalm 59:7, 15

Verses 6 and 14 are followed by descriptions of what these "dogs" do with their mouths.

❷ *What is meant by these images?*

Read Psalm 59:8, 16

These verses both start with a "but".

❷ *Why might God laugh at David's enemies in v 8? (See Psalm 2 for help!)*

❷ *Why is David able to sing in the face of such a brutal threat in Psalm 59:16?*

Read Psalm 59:9-10, 17

At the heart of the psalm are the repeated words of verses 9-10 and 17.

❷ *What truths does he recite about God, and how might this have helped him as he faced deadly enemies?*

✔ Apply

Whenever we read in the psalms about God's king, David, suffering at the hands of enemies, we hear echoes of the life of his descendant, King Jesus.

❷ *How does Jesus' experience of trusting God in the face of enemies make our understanding of this psalm richer?*

❷ *What particular lessons do you need to learn from this psalm when you are suffering due to the words of others?*

⌃ Pray

Bring before God the lives of Christians who are facing danger and persecution at the moment, and pray that they would know God in the way verses 9-10 and 14 describe him.

Bible in a year: 2 Corinthians 9 – 10

Sent by the Spirit

We now reach the second part of Luke's book. The spotlight shifts from Peter to Paul, whose gospel missions across the Roman Empire are the focus of the rest of Acts.

Sent

Read Acts 12:25 – 13:3

> ❓ *How had Saul become part of the church at Antioch? (See 11:25-26.)*

> ❓ *What was Barnabas and Saul's "mission" in Jerusalem (12:25—see 11:28-30)?*

> ❓ *Who returned from Jerusalem with Barnabas and Saul (12:25)?*

Barnabas is an extraordinary example of "a person of peace"—someone who has a knack for making lasting personal connections for the sake of the kingdom. (See Matthew 10:11 and Luke 10:6.)

Barnabas and Saul were part of a diverse group of prophets and teachers (Acts 13:1)—an African (Simeon), a Cyrenian (Lucius), and an aristocrat (Manean).

> ❓ *In what two activities did this group regularly engage (v 2)?*

> ❓ *What did the Spirit say to them (v 2)?*

> ❓ *In what four ways did the group respond (v 3)?*

Apply

Christian community is the best place to hear the voice of the Spirit.

> ❓ *With whom do you worship, fast and pray to prepare you to receive the Lord's guidance?*

Opposed

Read Acts 13:4-5

Barnabas, Saul and John Mark travelled 16 miles to Seleucia before taking a boat 130 miles to the island of Cyprus. Then they walked its length to Paphos (v 6).

> ❓ *What did they do on Cyprus?*

> ❓ *Where specifically did they do this?*

> ❓ *According to verse 3, who sent Barnabas and Saul? According to verse 4, who sent Barnabas and Saul? What does this teach us about the way God works?*

Read Acts 13:6-12

Paul's message inspired opposition from Bar-Jesus, aka Elymas.

> ❓ *What four charges did Paul level against him and what punishment did he receive (v 10-11)?*

> ❓ *What result did this have (v 12)?*

Notice again the complementary nature of words and deeds: this demonstration of God's power substantiated the truthfulness of God's message.

Pray

With whom are you seeking to share the message of God's love in Jesus? Ask God to open their hearts to the good news. Ask him to give you fresh ways to love them that would substantiate the gospel you share.

The message of salvation

Barnabas, Paul and John Mark left Cyprus by boat for Perga, 185 miles away. Then they headed another 100 miles inland to Pisidian Antioch to continue their mission.

Read Acts 13:13-15

Luke tells us about the evolving team dynamics on the journey.

> ❓ *By this point who emerged as the team's leader (v 13)?*

> ❓ *Who left the team (v 13)? Where did he go?*

Promise to the people

Yesterday we discovered that Paul and Barnabas went to synagogues to share the message about Jesus (v 5). Today Luke presents an extended example of what they said when they went there.

Read Acts 13:16-22

Paul recounts all the things that God did for the people of Israel.

> ❓ *What are they? Of the many things, which stand out to you? Why?*

> ❓ *All along the way, what did God promise to his people (v 23)?*

🔼 Pray

Give thanks to God for his unceasing grace that finds us and never gives up on us.

Saviour for the people

Read Acts 13:23-31

> ❓ *What did John the Baptist do to prepare the people for Jesus' arrival (v 24-25)?*

> ❓ *What was the people's response to Jesus (v 27-29)?*

> ❓ *How did God vindicate Jesus (v 30)?*

> ❓ *How did God spread the message about Jesus (v 31)?*

What you hold in your hands—the book of Acts and the New Testament—is the apostles' written witness to the resurrection of Jesus. Through their testimony God has given to you the "message of salvation" (v 26). All praise to our gracious God!

> ❓ *Paul's sermon gives us a clue as to why his team went to synagogues (v 27). What is that clue?*

Notice that Paul was certain that, no matter what Scriptures were being read, he could proclaim Jesus as the realisation of any and every biblical text. This should shape how we approach our own Bible reading, and any Bible teaching we have the privilege of doing—to see Jesus as the hero of every story, the fulfilment of every law, the culmination of every aspiration, and the way that God keeps all of his promises.

🔼 Pray

Spend some time thanking God for speaking to you in his word. Pray that the eyes of your heart would see Jesus, and be amazed by Jesus, whenever you read it.

Promises fulfilled

Sometimes it takes a while for good news—the end of a war, or the engagement of a friend, or the passing of an exam—to reach us. It was the same for Pisidian Antioch.

By raising up Jesus

In our last study, we read the first half of Paul's sermon at the synagogue in Pisidian Antioch. Today we hear his concluding declaration: *We have come with good news—the Messiah has come!*

Read Acts 13:32-37

Paul summarised the good news in three points (v 32-33):

- God made promises to our ancestors.
- God has fulfilled those promises for us.
- The means by which he has fulfilled them is the resurrection of Jesus.

To support those claims he quotes from the Old Testament three times. The first (v 33) is from Psalm 2, in which God announces to the world who his rightful son is.

❓ *According to Paul, what did God declare about Jesus on that first Easter Sunday?*

The second quotation (Acts 13:34) comes from Isaiah 55, where God invites everyone to drink freely of his mercy. Notably the word "you" is plural; the promises God gave to David are for "you all". The third quotation (Acts 13:35) is from Psalm 16, the same passage Peter proclaimed on the day of Pentecost.

···· TIME OUT ·······································

Compare Acts 13:36-37 with Acts 2:29-32 and look for similarities between these two expositions of Psalm 2.

⌄ Apply

Christians pay a lot of attention to what the cross accomplishes—and rightly so! But Paul argued that the resurrection of Jesus is every bit as important, for it is the means by which God has fulfilled his promises to you.

❓ *When is the last time you talked about, sang of, or gave thanks for the resurrection?*

He has fulfilled

Read Acts 13:38-41

❓ *What promise is given to us through Jesus, according to...*
   • *v 38?*   • *v 39?*

❓ *How are these two similar? What does the second statement add to the first?*

The sermon ends with a warning (v 40-41) taken from Habakkuk 1.

❓ *What did Paul say would happen to those who don't heed his warning?*

⌃ Pray

Spend some time thanking God for his promises, and for the fact that he never breaks or delays any of them. Recall particular promises and ask him to show you how to live by faith in them today.

The plan

Paul developed a strategy for sharing the gospel through the Roman Empire (which he details in Romans 15). Today's passage shows it being born.

To the city

Read Acts 13:42-45

❷ *How would you describe the response of the people to Paul and Barnabas's message (v 42)?*

From a single sermon, the message of the risen Messiah stretched across Pisidian Antioch. The anticipation reached such heights that just a week later "almost the whole city" came to hear them (v 44). Long before social media or cell phones, the gospel had gone viral!

❷ *What was the reaction of the religious authorities to their message (v 45)?*

To the Gentiles

Read Acts 13:46-48

❷ *What two charges did Paul and Barnabas level against the Jewish leaders (v 46)?*

❷ *What did Paul and Barnabas intend to do next (v 46)?*

Paul came to see that God had appointed him as "a minister of Christ Jesus to the Gentiles" (Romans 15:16). But this calling did not mean he stopped trying to share the good news with his fellow Jews (see Acts 14:1; 17:1)—nor that he stopped longing for them to come to faith in the Messiah (Romans 10:1).

To establish his claim as the apostle to the Gentiles, in Acts 13:47 Paul appealed to Isaiah's second Servant Song, found in Isaiah 49.

❷ *The "you" in Acts 13:47 is singular. Who is the "light for the Gentiles"?*

❷ *For what purpose did God make him a light for the Gentiles?*

⌃ Pray

Offer thanks to God that his mercy reaches to the ends of the earth. Ask him to empower his children—you!—to share Jesus with those who do not yet believe, wherever they are and wherever they are from.

To the whole region

Read Acts 13:49-52

Not for the last time, persecution has Paul and Barnabas on the move. But they left behind a band of disciples who "were filled with joy and with the Holy Spirit" (v 52).

By the time he wrote Romans, Paul could find "no more place for me to work in these regions", including the region around Pisidian Antioch (Romans 15:23). This was his strategy to reach the known world—to saturate cities with the message of Jesus, beginning at the synagogues, and then to let the new disciples spread it through the surrounding regions. That work is still continuing—through us, today.

Two different reactions

Paul and Barnabas head eastwards to two more cities in southern Galatia (in modern-day Turkey). The responses they find there couldn't be more different from each other!

The enemies are here!

Read Acts 14:1-7

❷ *Where did Paul and Barnabas begin their ministry (v 1)?*

❷ *What two results came from their work (v 1-2)?*

Luke says that Paul and Barnabas shared the gospel "effectively" (v 2). Since Luke connects their effective speaking with the "great number" of people who believed, at minimum Luke means their communication was persuasive.

❷ *What characteristics do you think make evangelism persuasive?*

Through our study of Acts we've noted the integration between proclamation (word ministry) and demonstration (deed ministry). In verse 3 Luke gives a clear explanation of the relationship between these two.

❷ *How does the Lord use these two in tandem?*

⌄ Apply

❷ *In what ways does your church express its faith through its deeds (see James 2:18)?*

❷ *In what ways can you help to confirm "the message of his grace" by loving your neighbours well?*

The gods are here!

Read Acts 14:8-10

As in Iconium, the missionaries' ministry in Lystra featured both speaking (v 9) and healing (v 10). When Luke says that Paul "saw that he had faith to be healed", he doesn't mean that the man had a visible aura about him, but that the Holy Spirit had given the apostle the sense that he was going to do something miraculous for him.

Read Acts 14:11-13

❷ *How did the people of Lystra interpret Paul's ability to heal (v 11)?*

❷ *What did the priest of Zeus want to do for Paul and Barnabas (v 13)?*

The Greek gods were unpredictable and required placating so that they did not grow angry. So this sacrifice would not have been motivated so much by thankfulness or love as worry and fear.

Read Acts 14:14-18

❷ *How did Paul and Barnabas describe the gods currently being worshipped (v 15)?*

❷ *How is the true God different to the Greek gods (v 15-17)?*

⌃ Pray

Spend time praising God for who he is. Let the comparison with the false Greek gods inform your praise.

Suffering and strengthening

Imagine you're on trial for a crime you didn't commit. Every witness has fabricated incriminating stories. The judge is furious with you. And now it's your turn to speak.

Pressing ahead

Read Acts 14:19-21

❓ *Paul's persecutors "came from Antioch and Iconium". What does this tell you about their opposition to the gospel?*

The crowd they won over is the same crowd we saw in verse 11.

❓ *What insight does that give you into human nature?*

❓ *What did they try to do to Paul, and to what extent did they think they had succeeded?*

❓ *Why is what Paul did next amazing?*

❓ *What was the impact in Derbe (v 21)?*

Pray

Not every Christian suffers for their faith the same way Paul did, but some do, and all of us should be ready. Ask God to enable you to live wisely, courageously, and humbly, regardless of circumstance, so that Jesus may be known through you.

Doubling back

In Derbe Paul and Barnabas reached the end of their Galatian journey. But instead of continuing on towards home, they retraced their steps and revisited each city in reverse order.

Read Acts 14:21b-25

❓ *How had they left ...*
- *Pisidian Antioch (13:50-51)?*
- *Iconium (14:5-6)?*
- *Lystra (14:19)?*

❓ *What do verses 22-23 suggest was the reason they revisited these churches instead of heading straight home?*

The last phrase of verse 23 ("in whom they had put their trust") is a powerful reminder that, as much as we trust Christian leaders and even the apostles themselves, ultimately our hope is in Jesus. We rightly praise God for elders who lead well, but at the end of the day there is only one Saviour in whom we put our trust.

Apply

❓ *To what degree does your expectation of the Christian life match Paul and Barnabas's description of it in verse 22?*

❓ *How can you make sure you have a clear view of the future kingdom you'll experience, to enable you to face hardship with joy in the present?*

Heading home

Read Acts 14:26-28

Finally the missionary team of Paul and Barnabas head home to Syrian Antioch.

❓ *How do you think that church felt when they heard the mission report?*

Bible in a year: Luke 3 – 4

God's megaphone

Let's be honest: you don't see many Christian bookmarks with verse 8 on them! How do you react when you come to places in the Bible that just seem incomprehensible?

This psalm talks about places we've never been to in a way that we don't understand, and so we're tempted to skip it and move on. But why not stay around and see why the Holy Spirit ensured this quirky little psalm found its way into our Bibles…?

Context

According to 2 Samuel 8, while the Israelite army was away fighting near the Euphrates, their neighbours in Edom took the opportunity to attack their unprotected lands.

Read Psalm 60:1-5

❷ *Who does David see is ultimately sovereign over Israel's military defeat in verses 1-3?*

❷ *So to whom does he turn to for help in verses 4-5?*

Read Psalm 60:6-8

❷ *We may not be familiar with all the imagery in verses 6-8, but what is going on?*

❷ *What might be a modern way to describe God's triumphant behaviour?*

Read Psalm 60:9-12

❷ *Where might David have been tempted to turn for help, given that God seems to have rejected the Israelites?*

❷ *Where instead does he turn, according to verses 9-12?*

The logic here is important for us too: if God rejects us, then our only hope is… it's still God! God is still almighty even when things go against us. Humans are still only created things, no matter how high they rise in this life. So we would be fools to put our trust anywhere but in God our Saviour.

⬇ Apply

C.S. Lewis described suffering as "God's megaphone" to rouse a deaf world. As you look back on your life, do you find that disappointment, discouragement and suffering drive you to God in dependence, or away from him in bitterness?

❷ *Why do you think that is?*

⬆ Pray

Praise God that he fights for his people. Colossians 2:15 describes Jesus' death on the cross as his triumph. On the cross he *"tossed his sandal"* upon sin and the devil, and in his resurrection, he *"shouted in triumph"* over death.

Pray that hard times would not drive you away from God in bitterness and disappointment but drive you to God in desperation and dependence.

Bible in a year: 2 Corinthians 11 – 13

Faith or faith plus law?

Some churches (and Christians) allow disputes over minor matters to become heated. That's not what's going on here—here, the truth of the gospel is genuinely at stake.

The dispute

Read Acts 15:1-5

❓ *What condition did these teachers impose on the church (v 1, 5)?*

❓ *What did they say was the penalty for not complying (v 1)?*

Circumcision was God's idea (Genesis 17). So these teachers seemed to have a biblical basis for making it a condition for salvation. That is what gave their argument its force.

❓ *To whom did the church appeal for counsel (Acts 15:2)?*

❓ *What stories did Paul and Barnabas share along the way (v 3) and in Jerusalem (v 4)?*

❓ *What effect did these stories have on the hearers (v 3-4)?*

The discussion

Luke highlights three witnesses whose testimony won the day: an apostle, a missionary team and an elder.

Read Acts 15:6-11

❓ *How had God shown that he accepted the Gentiles (v 8)?*

Read Acts 15:12

❓ *What did Paul and Barnabas tell the apostles and elders?*

As we've seen, they ministered both in word and in deed. Here, they focus on the latter—because this was a supernatural sign of God's acceptance of Gentiles who turned to Jesus in faith.

Read Acts 15:13-18

❓ *To what did James appeal (v 15)?*

❓ *What promise did God give (v 17)?*

Along with the coming of the Spirit and the doing of signs and wonders, the final proof that God accepts people apart from the law is the Old Testament.

The decision

Read Acts 15:19-21

❓ *What was the decision on the question of circumcision (v 19)?*

❓ *What four recommendations did they present (v 20)?*

We should read their counsel not as new laws but as a guide for these converts to live faithfully in a pagan society (with which they were quite familiar) among Jewish-background believers (with whom they were not).

🔼 Pray

It is easy to grow familiar with the truth that God accepts us on the basis of Jesus' faith and not our law-keeping. But it is a radical and wonderful truth. Pause to think about it, and then praise God for it.

 Bible in a year: Exodus 29 – 32

A good news letter

The decision has been made. Faith in Jesus is all that is necessary to be accepted by God. Now the decision needs to be communicated to the churches.

The messengers

Read Acts 15:22

❷ Who made the decision to send representatives to Syrian Antioch (v 22)?

❷ What do we learn about Judas Barsabbas and Silas in v 22? In v 32?

The message

Read Acts 15:23-29

The apostles and elders began by expressing deep concern. Those advocating a return to the Mosaic Law had harmed the church at Antioch in two ways: they disturbed the believers and troubled their minds by what they said (v 23).

❷ What does the apostles' example teach us about faithful pastoral ministry?

Again, we see the apostles taking care neither to teach that our behaviour can save us, nor that our behaviour is unimportant. There were areas in which the Christians receiving this letter "will do well" to act in certain ways, out of sensitivity to Jewish Christians and out of a desire to reach out to Jewish people. But there is a world of difference between something we "will do well" to do, and something we *must* do in order to be, or to remain, acceptable to God.

☑ Apply

❷ Can you think of any ways in which you're tempted either to think certain behaviours are necessary in order to be a Christian; or unimportant to pursue as a Christian?

The response

Read Acts 15:30-35

These verses teem with words—the words of the letter and the words of God.

❷ Find all the things people did with these words.

❷ Find all the effects that these words had on the people.

It's easy to think that word ministry is only for super Christians like Paul and Barnabas. That's why I love the phrase "many others" in verse 35. It's a subtle reminder that the Spirit equips lots of people to share God's good news in Jesus with believers and non-believers alike.

☑ Apply

What ministry of the word is God calling you to do? Are you being prompted to do more in some way or to start seeking to teach God's word in a new way?

Bible in a year: 2 Samuel 20 – 24

A difficult parting

After the resolution to the crucial dispute over what is required to be acceptable to God, the peace is quickly broken by a new disagreement.

Sadly this one is between two men who had both "risked their lives for the name of our Lord Jesus Christ" (v 26).

The plan

Read Acts 15:36

On their first journey, Paul and Barnabas had traversed Cyprus before heading north into the cities of Galatia, starting churches wherever they went (Acts 13 – 14).

❷ *What two things did Paul want to accomplish on this second journey (15:36)?*

The disagreement

Read Acts 15:37-38

Let's review what we know about John Mark.

❷ *Where was he from (12:25)?*

❷ *What part had he played on the first journey (13:5)?*

❷ *What had happened (13:13)? Where did he go?*

One key to understanding sharp disagreements is the word "wise" (15:38). Wisdom refers to skilfully accomplishing God's will in any given situation. We grow in wisdom over time as we know and experience God in more and new ways (Proverbs 9:10; Luke 2:52). But because wisdom grows over time, different people with different experiences

at different stages of life often see the same issue in different ways, even though both love and follow Jesus. That's what happened to Paul and Barnabas; one considered a path wise, the other did not.

The split

Read Acts 15:39-41

❷ *Who set out to fulfil the original vision for the trip by going to Cyprus (v 39)?*

❷ *Whose journey does Luke follow for the rest of the book (v 40)?*

❷ *Who received the church's commendation (v 40)?*

❷ *What did Paul say about John Mark in his final letter (2 Timothy 4:11)?*

Who was right? Luke makes that answer difficult to discern. But it is a reminder that sometimes disagreements do come. Sometimes Christians cannot work together. But neither of these two men allowed the disagreement to sidetrack them from their work God had called them to. Neither should we.

⌃ Pray

Ask God for the ability to discern the difference between a dispute about the gospel and one about wisdom; the patience to listen well; the humility to change your mind or the courage to gently stand your ground; and the wisdom to know which to do in each situation.

Into Europe

Paul had intended to go with Barnabas to Cyprus, but now was going on foot to Galatia with Silas. And yet the detours were only just beginning...

Growing churches

Read Acts 16:1-5

Timothy's circumcision might come as a surprise, given Paul's vehement objection to the circumcision-insisting teachers in the previous chapter. To understand his reasoning, **read 1 Corinthians 9:19-23.**

❓ *What was his ultimate goal when making decisions like this (v 22)?*

Paul wanted to visit the Galatian churches in order to "see how they [were] doing" (Acts 15:36).

❓ *What did he discover (16:5)?*

🔼 Pray

Ask the Holy Spirit to make these two qualities—being strengthened in the faith and growing daily in numbers—a reality for your church.

Wandering missionaries

Read Acts 16:6-8

❓ *What did Paul and his team try to do?*

❓ *Why couldn't they?*

We don't know how the Holy Spirit prevented them. Maybe they had an inner sense. Maybe they saw a vision. Maybe circumstances were ordered in such a way they could not continue. We simply don't know. What we do know is that they weren't able to do what they planned to do, and that the Spirit was the reason they couldn't.

Opening hearts

Read Acts 16:9-15

❓ *Why did the team end up in Philippi (v 9-10)?*

The gospel began in Jerusalem in Asia, spread to Africa (Acts 8), and now, for the first time, it crosses into Europe.

"They" (Acts 16:8) shifts to "we" (v 10).

❓ *Who must have joined the team at this point?*

❓ *Who came to faith, and what does verse 14 tell us about how people become Christians?*

❓ *What does verse 15 show are two right responses to joining God's family?*

❓ *How do you think Paul would have reflected at this point on the frustration of his plans that he'd experienced in Asia?*

🔽 Apply

❓ *How does this story guide your response to frustrations that you experience in your life, your plans, or your work?*

Talk to the Spirit and ask him for direction, for patience and for growth. And pray that he would guide you to a Lydia today, who is ready to hear the gospel and respond.

Bible in a year: Job 41 – 42

A slave and a jailer

During Paul's first missionary journey a pattern emerged: he preached in a synagogue, the message spread from there, people came to faith, and persecution followed.

But Philippi had no synagogue. So "on the Sabbath" he went to "a place of prayer" (v 13)—and Lydia believed. It was a slight adjustment to the pattern; still, everything was going according to plan. Until…

The girl

Read Acts 16:16-18

❓ *What are we told about this young woman?*

❓ *What did she say about Paul and his team, and for how long (v 17-18)?*

❓ *How did Paul respond (v 18)?*

One sign of the authenticity of the New Testament is that it "tells on" its heroes. It doesn't pretend that Paul is superhuman.

······ TIME OUT ··································

❓ *Why didn't Paul cast out the demon sooner, do you think? (Hint: review the pattern from Paul's first missionary journey. What did he expect would happen once the gospel "went public"?)*

The accusation

Read Acts 16:19-24

❓ *What motivated the slave owners to arrest Paul and Silas (v 19)?*

❓ *What charges did they level against them (v 20-21)? Were any of these true?*

The cross and resurrection of Jesus undermine every idolatry of the human heart. The longing for approval, the lust for power, the desire for success, the craving for pleasure—these lose their power in the face of the risen Jesus. So it is no surprise that the triumph of the gospel in Philippi should result in slaveowners losing money. The gospel upends human greed and systems of oppression.

✅ Apply

❓ *What are the particular idols worshipped in your own city or community? How does the gospel confront and upend them?*

❓ *What will look different in your life because you love and serve Jesus, not those idols?*

The intervention

Read Acts 16:25-31

Compare this scene with Peter's experience in Acts 12:6-10.

❓ *What is similar about the accounts? What is different?*

The gospel is good news—not advice, not a new law, but news about Jesus, his life, death, and resurrection. News like this demands only one response: believe (16:31).

Last night in Philippi

The story of what happened in that Philippian jail is so encouraging that we'll look at it again today!

Singing praise

Read Acts 16:25-29

It's striking that Luke describes the earthquake as "violent" (v 26) so soon after Paul and Silas's violent treatment by the magistrates of Philippi.

❓ *Look back at v 22-24. How many expressions of violence against Paul and Silas do you find in these three verses?*

❓ *In between their violent treatment and the violent earthquake, what were Paul and Silas doing (v 25)?*

⌃ Pray

With bruised bodies, broken bones and shackled feet, Paul and Silas expressed a kind of joy, peace and gentleness that comes only from the Spirit of God (Galatians 5:22-23). Ask the Lord to assure you by his Spirit that "our present sufferings are not worth comparing with the glory that will be revealed in us" (Romans 8:18).

Bringing hope

Read Acts 16:30-34

❓ *What did Paul and Silas do for the jailer and his household?*

❓ *When did all of this happen?*

❓ *Why was the jailer filled with joy?*

The longer someone follows Jesus, the greater the temptation to be cynical about a new convert's joy. We've been around the gospel for so long that it can lose its wonder. So take a moment to reflect on it now—that simply by believing, you have been saved and united to Christ, adopted into the Father's family, indwelled by the Spirit, and looking forward with certainty to an eternity spent enjoying and praising our God.

⌄ Apply

One of Paul's last instructions to his co-labourer Timothy was to "preach the word" even when it is "out of season"—that is, inconvenient (2 Timothy 4:2). This situation sure qualifies!

❓ *What steps can you take now to be prepared to share Jesus even when it's inconvenient?*

Decrying injustice

Read Acts 16:35-40

❓ *What was Paul's accusation against the "officers" (v 37)?*

❓ *How did the magistrates handle their accusation (v 39)? Was justice served?*

Note that Paul and Silas didn't take this opportunity to evangelise. Their focus was on calling out an obvious injustice. Sometimes this is the best way to bear witness to Jesus. *Are there injustices that you need to stand or speak against? What will that look like?*

Bible in a year: Luke 5 – 6

Rock, wing, king

The rock, the wing, and the king: not a bonus round from a scavenger hunt. But the three things God provides that give David comfort and hope in the face of danger.

The rock

Read Psalm 61:1-3

> ❷ *How does David describe God in v 2-3?*
> ❷ *When have you found God to be a rock, a refuge or a strong tower in your life?*

The most important thing about this rock of refuge appears at the end of v 2—it is "higher than I". We like to be self-sufficient and to think that we can make it through life trusting in our abilities. But sometimes we find ourselves in real trouble facing things that we cannot deal with. At that point it is an enormous relief to know that when we turn to God, we turn to a rock that is "higher than I". His wisdom, his love and his mercy are infinitely more powerful than anything we could muster up ourselves.

The wing

Read Psalm 61:4

The picture changes in verse 4. Here is something altogether more gentle. As David turns to God he finds more than just mighty power. He also finds gentle care. God gathers him to himself like a mother hen, protecting a vulnerable chick under its wings.

⌄ Apply

> ❷ *How would it change the help God gave us if the Bible only ever pictured him as providing a solid rock, and never a comforting wing?*
> ❷ *What if it was the other way around?*

The king

Read Psalm 61:5-8

It might seem strange that David should all of a sudden pray for God's protection of his king (v 5-8). However, he knew that the fate of God's people is tied to the fate of their king. When the kings of Israel were faithful and victorious, the people were godly and prosperous. When the kings ignored God, the people turned away from God and suffered.

It was true for them, but how much more so for us if we trust in Jesus! God's Messiah is not just our king who leads us, but by faith we are united to him—we are "in him", as the New Testament says over 150 times. That means we share in his victory, his righteousness, his eternal life and his perfect relationship with God. David prayed for long life and victory for the king. We praise God that he answered David's prayer in the death and resurrection of Jesus Christ.

⌃ Pray

Praise God for the way that David's prayer for his king has been answered in Jesus.

Pray for deep understanding of God's rock-solid protection, and his gentle, kindly care.

Two more cities

Paul and Silas continued their journey across ancient Greece until they came across a familiar sight—"a Jewish synagogue" (v 1), the first they'd encountered in Europe.

They knew what to do next!

Persuading some

Read Acts 17:1-4

❓ What did Paul do in the synagogue in Thessalonica (v 2)?

❓ What points was he trying to make (v 3)?

❓ What was the basis of his argument (v 2)?

Apply

❓ If someone asked you to prove that Jesus must suffer and rise from the dead, using only the Old Testament, would you be able to do it?

❓ Which point would you find easier to prove: his suffering or his resurrection?

For further reflection on this question, review Acts 2:25-28; 8:32-33; 13:32-35.

Facing the backlash

Read Acts 17:5-9

In every age there are "bad characters" waiting around to form a mob and start a riot (v 5). In ancient Thessalonica they were in the marketplace; in our day they're harder to spot.

···· TIME OUT ··

Think about the media you consume and the feeds you read.

❓ Are there individuals/outlets that always seem ready to form a mob and start a riot?

❓ Do you need to stop them from speaking into your views and life?

···

❓ What did Jason do "wrong" (v 7)?

❓ How did he pay for it (v 6, 9)?

Jealousy (v 5) is an emotion that we experience when a seeming rival threatens a valued relationship. It's powerful, self-justifying and destructive—as we see here.

Winning many

Read Acts 17:10-12

❓ Why does Luke say the Berean Jews possessed a "more noble character" (v 11)?

❓ What was the result (v 12)?

The example of the Berean Jews instructs us to approach the Scriptures with humility. They were already diligent students... yet there was more to learn. We must be careful not to read into the Bible our preconceived notions, subtly refusing to allow it to surprise us or to change our thinking.

Pray

Ask the Spirit to grant you humility and to "guide you into all the truth" (John 16:13) as you search the Scriptures.

The gospel in Athens

Persecution was now meeting Paul at almost every turn. Again he was forced to leave a city, this time Berea. So he found himself heading south, to Athens.

Moving

Read Acts 17:13-15

Through all of his journeys Paul worked with teams. But sometimes God leaves his servants to carry on their work alone.

Apply

❓ *Can you think of a time when God called you to go it alone? What did he teach you about himself during that time? What fruit did he bear in you and others through that season?*

Waiting

Sometimes we wish we could get on with our plans yet we're delayed. But God has good things for us in the waiting.

Read Acts 17:16-21

❓ *In what two places did Paul share the good news of Jesus (v 17)? Whom did he seek to reach there?*

❓ *What specific message did he proclaim to the philosophers (v 18)?*

❓ *What three responses did he provoke (v 18-19)?*

Epicureans believed that the goal of life was happiness and the absence of pain.

❓ *How would "the good news about Jesus and the resurrection" challenge their system of belief?*

Stoics believed that the goal of life was self-control and the mastery of destructive emotions.

❓ *How would "the good news about Jesus and the resurrection" challenge their system of belief?*

Observing

Read Acts 17:22-23

❓ *What had Paul noticed during his time waiting in Athens?*

❓ *What offer or promise was he making to his listeners?*

Paul had taken the time to understand those whom he wished to understand the gospel. And this informed how he shared that gospel with them. The Athenians knew there was another God they ought to worship, but they knew that they didn't know who he was. Notice how different this opening is to his evangelism to Jews who knew their Old Testaments (e.g. 13:16-19).

Apply

Think about the hopes and dreams and frustrations of people who live in your neighbourhood or work in your office, and of your wider culture.

❓ *How could this shape the way you talk about the gospel with them, so that you connect with them where they are at?*

Bible in a year: 1 Kings 1 – 4

Not that—instead, this

Paul's speech to the most prominent figures in Athens was given in the shadow of the Acropolis, their great centre of religious worship. His message? Not that—instead, this.

Who needs whom?

Pay close attention to the repeated word "not" in his sermon. Each time Paul used it to differentiate false belief with the truth about God.

Read Acts 17:24-28

- ❓ *What two false ideas about God did Paul refute in v 24-25?*
- ❓ *What did these false ideas wrongly assert about God (v 25)?*

Paul asserted that the opposite is actually true—that human existence depends on God.

- ❓ *How many different ways did Paul make this point (v 25-26)?*

Paul flipped the philosophers' idea on its head, subverting their misguided notion that God needs humans. In its place he restored a radically theocentric (God-centred) vision of the universe, where we are the ones in need of him.

This address is unlike any other sermon in Acts. Not only is there no explicit quotation from the Bible, the two quotations found in verse 28 are from Greek philosophers.

- ❓ *Why do you think Paul cited them instead of Scripture? How does this example shed light on how we share the message of Jesus with others?*

Who reflects whom?

Read Acts 17:29-31

Trace Paul's reasoning in verse 29. Humans have the capacity for creativity, for communication, for relationship, for consciousness itself. Since we are God's offspring, these things and more must come from him. In other words, humans are made in God's image, not the other way around.

- ❓ *What is the only right response to the truths about God and about humans that Paul had laid out (v 30)?*
- ❓ *What is Paul's final argument to validate his words (v 31)?*

Pray

Take Paul's exhortation in verse 30 to heart right now. Pause for a moment and ask his Spirit to examine your heart. Acknowledge whatever he turns up, turn away from it, and seek forgiveness in Jesus' name.

How will you respond?

Read Acts 17:32-34

- ❓ *What three responses did Paul's message provoke?*
- ❓ *How might that be a helpful way to set our expectations in our own conversations about Jesus with those around us?*

SONG OF SONGS: Love

What's your favourite love song? What makes it so special? The lyrics? The tune? Or perhaps because you associate it with the one you love?

Read Song of Songs 1:1-4

❓ *Who is speaking?*

❓ *What requests do they make?*

The poem opens with "Let him kiss me" (v 2). It's a call to love. This song celebrates the joy of love and sex within marriage, along with recounting the heartache of unfulfilled longing. But there's more to it than this...

This poem also speaks of God's love for his people and the intimacy he seeks with believers. This is true because God designed marriage to be a picture of Christ's love for the church. But there are other reasons to think that this link is intended by the writer.

1. The woman is likened to the land of Israel, often in ways that don't seem to work as descriptions of human beauty. Is she like Israel or is Israel like a bride? The poem works on both levels. In Isaiah 62:4, God promises, "Your land will be married".

2. The poem is full of garden imagery that takes us back to the Garden of Eden. The poem describes the restoration of the intimacy of Eden that was lost when humanity rebelled against God.

3. The woman is likened to a vineyard, just as God likens Israel to a vineyard (Isaiah 5:1-7).

The greatest love

This poem claims to be the "Song of Songs" (Song of Songs 1:1). It's a way of saying it's the greatest song (just as the "Holy of holies" in the temple was the most holy place). That's a bold claim. Is it really better than all of Solomon's thousand other songs (1 Kings 4:32)?

Yes—this is the greatest song because it celebrates the greatest *love*: the love of Christ for the church. Seeing his love in his word is like receiving a kiss from his mouth (Song of Songs 1:2).

As we walk through this wonderful poem, we'll keep the human lovers we meet there in mind; but it's the love between Christ and his church that will be our focus in these studies.

⌄ Apply

❓ *What signs of Christ's love ("his kisses") have you experienced recently?*

❓ *Why is his love "delightful" (v 2) to you today?*

❓ *In what way is his name "pleasing" (v 3) to you today?*

⌃ Pray

Turn verses 2-4 into an expression of your longing for Jesus.

How beautiful are you?

Without us realising it, our perceptions of beauty are partly linked to wealth and status.

For instance, white Western people often want a tan because in the West darker skin can suggest the leisure to go sunbathing.

In Solomon's day, dark skin was unattractive because it signified a peasant who worked in the sun. The woman singer is what some might call today a "redneck" (v 5-6).

Do not stare at me

Read Song of Songs 1:5-6

❓ *How does this woman regard herself?*

In verse 6 she feels the critical stares of the fashionable city girls—just as today we imagine people rating our social-media posts. She's had to neglect her figurative vineyard (her attractiveness) to work in her family's literal vineyards (v 6). Like so many people today, she feels insecure about her appearance.

How beautiful you are

Read Song of Songs 1:7-17

Although she pictures her beloved as her "king" (v 4, 12), he's actually a young shepherd—so she looks for him among the flocks (v 7-8). There the young lovers spend time together on a bed of green foliage with branches forming a roof over their heads (v 16-17). Whenever we spend time listening to Christ's voice in his word and responding in prayer we're spending time enjoying the love of our Beloved (see also v 4).

❓ *How does the man she loves regard her in these verses?*

Verse 9 may not be the best chat-up line to use today! (The jewellery listed in verses 10-11 suggests that verse 9 is a reference to her adornments rather than her physical features.) But his feelings for her are clear in verse 15: "How beautiful you are, my darling!"

Read Ephesians 5:25-27

❓ *What has Christ done for his bride, the church?*

❓ *What is he doing for his bride?*

❓ *What will be the result of his work?*

❤ Apply

❓ *How do you regard yourself?*

❓ *What makes you feel insecure about your identity?*

Perhaps you feel the scrutiny of other people. You imagine them judging your appearance or your performance at work or your commitment to the church. What about the scrutiny of God? Nothing can be hidden from him and his standard is perfection (Hebrews 4:13).

And yet this is what Jesus says to you: "How beautiful you are, my darling!" He looks beyond our sin to see his bride. He sees the beauty he is creating in you.

❓ *What do you want to say to him?*

Bible in a year: Jeremiah 47 – 52

Don't settle for less

Imagine you find a magic lamp. You give it a rub and a genie appears, offering you one wish. What would you wish for?

Today, the Song invites us not to settle for anything less than true love.

You're the one for me

Read Song of Songs 2:1-3

"I am a rose of Sharon" (v 1) is not a boast. Our female singer is saying that she's a common flower, like any of the many flowers in the valleys. In my locality it would be like saying, "I'm just another buttercup in a field of buttercups. There are thousands of beautiful women in the world, so what makes me so special?" But she is special to her beloved: "a lily among thorns" (v 2). There may be thousands of beautiful women, but there's only one woman for him.

And she feels the same way about him. There may be thousands of other men ("trees of the forest" v 3), but she only wants to live under his care ("sit in his shade") and enjoy his love ("his fruit is sweet to my taste").

⌄ Apply

❷ *Is Jesus the only one for you? Do you look to other "trees" for protection?*

❷ *Does other "fruit" seem sweeter than Jesus? What, and why?*

Yes, but not yet

Read Song of Songs 2:4-7

These verses are an expression of desire.

She looks forward with longing to their wedding day (v 4-5) and wedding night (v 6). But she warns that these passions must not be awakened until the right time (v 7; see also 3:5; 8:4). Perhaps she is asking the city girls not to exert any unhelpful peer pressure.

⌄ Apply

❷ *Whatever your current "relationship status", how are you doing all you can to avoid arousing love with the wrong person or at the wrong time, so that sexual love is kept within marriage?*

❷ *In what ways are you most strongly tempted to do the opposite?*

Don't fool about

We were created with desires by God, to lead us to true fulfilment in Christ. But we very easily get diverted and settle for lesser joys. So 2:7 is a reminder not to settle for anything less than joy in Christ. As C.S. Lewis famously said, "We are half-hearted creatures, fooling about with drink and sex and ambition when infinite joy is offered to us. We are like an ignorant child who wants to go on making mud pies in the slum because he cannot imagine what is meant by the offer of a holiday at the sea. We are too easily pleased."

⌃ Pray

Pray for a heart that is satisfied only by Jesus, so that it can be satisfied completely by Jesus.

Rest in peace

At the heart of this psalm is a man who is harassed, persecuted and outnumbered. And yet he is at peace. His soul is at rest. How can this be? Read on to find out…

A wobbly fence and a mighty fortress

Read Psalm 62:1-4

It starts with a great declaration of trust in verses 1-2.

> ❷ *How does David describe God? By contrast, how confident is he in his own strength, in verses 3-4?*

A rock for all

Read Psalm 62:5-8

David now speaks to himself. He knows how wobbly he is, but he doesn't listen to his feelings and doubts. Instead he speaks truth about God to himself. Read verses 5-8 again. It does not matter how weak David is, he is leaning on God—a mighty concrete pillar to brace his tottering fence! But God is not just a dependable fortress for David, as verse 8 makes clear. There is room for all of us to shelter within his walls.

Finding security

Read Psalm 62:9-12

As so often in the psalms, David shows how wise we are to trust in God by comparing the alternatives. First there is human power and human attempts to find security.

> ❷ *How dependable does that sound in v 9-10?*

Then in verses 11-12, by contrast, he lists three wonderful characteristics of God that he is able to cling to.

> ❷ *What are they?*
> ❷ *How might they help his soul be at peace as he waits for God to deliver him?*

One of the great things about internet shopping is that you don't have to buy anything without having read dozens of reviews first. David wants us to read his review and so be encouraged to make God our refuge too.

⌄ Apply

Are you good at resting in God? Are you able to be at peace when you are facing financial worries? When the kids are going off the rails? When family relationships are a source of pain and tension? For most of us the answer to that is no! According to Paul, it is Jesus Christ who provides that peace (Philippians 4:7), and it is his Holy Spirit who alone can drive the truths of Psalm 62:1-2 into our hearts.

⌃ Pray

Pray that God would gently teach you a deeper trust, through small tests that prepare you for greater challenges.

Pray too that in unsettling times you would be better at focusing on truths about God, rather than doubts about yourself.

Bible in a year: Galatians 4 – 6

Come to Christ

You clearly attach some importance to reading the Bible and praying day by day, since here you are reading these notes. But how important is this moment to Christ?

Christ comes to you

Read Song of Songs 2:8-9, 17

The beloved comes to the woman, bounding like a gazelle because he is energised by his love. Picture Christ bounding towards you, energised by love, whenever he sees you opening your Bible.

Come to Christ

Read Song of Songs 2:10-14

Winter has passed and the world is coming into bloom with the arrival of spring. The implication is that now is the time for love to blossom. The longing will soon be over. The cold nights spent waiting will be replaced by the warmth of love. Twice we hear, "Come with me" (v 10, 13).

Apply

In the busyness of our lives and the noise of a godless world, Jesus comes to us with these words: "Arise, come, my darling; my beautiful one, come with me ... Show me your face, let me hear your voice" (v 10, 14). It's an invitation to spend time with him, hearing his love in the words of Scripture and responding with love in the words of our prayers. It's an invitation to his bride, the church, to hear him as we gather each Sunday. It's an invitation to step out of the cold and feel the warmth of his love.

Beware of the foxes

Read Song of Songs 2:15

"The little foxes" might sound cute, but they "ruin the vineyards". Perhaps rats would be a more redolent image today. Remember, too, that in the Song the "vineyard" is an image of sexuality, a place of intimacy (8:12). This verse calls on the wider community to protect young women from "love rats" who would use and abuse them. For Christians, in our relationship with Jesus the foxes represent anything that threatens our enjoyment of Christ by drawing us away from our true love.

Apply

- ❓ *What stops you coming to Christ each day?*
- ❓ *What distracts you when you spend time enjoying Christ in prayer?*

Ask God to protect you from these distractions.

He is mine

Read Song of Songs 2:16

Meditate on what it means to say, "Christ belongs to me". Then think deeply about what it means to say, "I belong to Christ".

Now turn your thoughts into prayers to him.

Pursue the one you love

What do we do when Christ seems distant?

It's easy to do nothing when we feel spiritually dry. But that only makes matters worse. These verses show us a better way.

Read Song of Songs 3:1-3

"All night long on my bed" (v 1) suggests that these verses may be a kind of dream sequence. Or they may be a flashback to a stylised version of their courtship and betrothal.

I looked for him

Re-read Song of Songs 3:1-3

❓ *Pick out all the actions the woman takes in these verses.*

She's not passive. She takes the initiative to find her beloved. But instead of finding him, she's found by the watchmen. So she gets them involved in the search (v 3).

⌄ Apply

A time when Christ seems distant is not a time to be passive. We need some "get up ... and go" (v 2). We need to look for him: in his word as we read it day by day, and among his people as we join with them week by week. We may also need to ask for help.

❓ *Is there something you need to do to pursue Christ?*

❓ *Is there someone you could ask to help you?*

I held him

Read Song of Songs 3:4

❓ *What does the woman do when she finds her beloved?*

She may be bringing him home in order to arrange their wedding. This time, she's going to hold on to him and not let him go.

There's a promise for us in these verses: "I looked for the one my heart loves ... I found the one my heart loves" (v 1, 4). Times of spiritual dryness are part of most Christian lives—we don't live on a constant emotional high. But Christ is not hiding from us. "Seek and you will find," he assures us (Matthew 7:7).

Read Song of Songs 3:5

Perhaps this renewed exhortation is prompted by what the watchmen have been saying, which may have been something like, *Why look for an absent lover when there are other suitable bachelors at hand?* "There are plenty more fish in the sea," we might say today. But there's only one man to whom she will give her love, and she will not give herself to him until they are bound together in the covenant of marriage.

⌃ Pray

Lord, may I have eyes only for you, so that all the other things I love are part of my love for you rather than rivals to my love for you. Amen.

Bible in a year: 1 Kings 5 – 9

Wedding bells

At the beginning of a wedding the bride makes her big entrance. That's what we see here.

Who's her king?

Read Song of Songs 3:6-11

❓ *How does the bride describe her beloved?*

I think the beloved is almost certainly not Solomon—not least because the Song ends by comparing the way the woman has protected "her vineyard" (her sexuality) to the way Solomon rented his out (by having numerous wives and concubines—1 Kings 11:1-3). The link between Solomon and the Song in Song of Songs 1:1 need not mean the Song is about him or by him. It could have been commissioned by Solomon or associated with the golden age of wisdom over which he presided.

So who is this? It's her shepherd-lover, whom she's already described as her "king" (1:4, 12).

❓ *If this is not actually Solomon, what effect does the bride achieve by describing her wedding, and her husband-to-be, in this way?*

Perhaps she's still dreaming, and in her dreams she imagines a fairy-tale wedding in which she marries her prince (3:1). Or perhaps this is an exaggerated description of their marriage, highlighting the way she considers him to be the greatest of men. He sends a noble bodyguard and luxurious carriage so she can travel to her wedding in safety and comfort.

Our Shepherd-King

Perhaps it's no accident that the beloved is a king-like shepherd. It reminds us of the Lord whom David describes as "my shepherd" (Psalm 23:1). It reminds us of David himself, the shepherd boy who became Israel's greatest king (2 Samuel 5:1-2). And it points forward to David's greater son, Jesus. Jesus is the King who came to be the good Shepherd, who laid down his life for his sheep (John 10:11).

The column of smoke in Song of Songs 3:6 is perfumed with "incense"—it's literally "frankincense". Yet incense couldn't be used as personal perfume because it only releases its scent when burnt. It was, however, used in the tabernacle. Indeed, that was the only place where it was to be used (Exodus 30:34-38). In the tabernacle, burning incense reminded the people of God's coming to his people in the clouds of Mount Sinai and leading them by means of the pillar of cloud. Now in Song of Songs 3:6, a pillar of cloud is coming through the wilderness to lead a bride to her wedding. This marriage is a picture of God redeeming his people, making a covenant with us and leading us home.

☑ Apply

❓ *How does all this imagery excite you about being loved by, and in love with, King Jesus?*

You've stolen my heart

Chapter 3 described the wedding of the two lovers. In chapter 4, we see them on their wedding night.

Read Song of Songs 4:1-11

How beautiful you are

If you didn't read these verses aloud, then do so now (though you might want to be careful who overhears you!).

- ❓ *How does the beloved praise his wife's beauty (v 1-7)?*
- ❓ *How does he feel about her love for him (v 8-10)?*
- ❓ *How does he describe her kisses (v 11)?*

The language is tender yet powerful. It's erotic and sensual without ever being smutty. It includes language we've heard before (compare 4:1 and 1:15, and 4:10 and 1:2-3). But now this is taken to another level because the couple have arrived at the wedding night. The restraint they have previously shown (2:7; 3:5) is no longer needed. Her hair is no longer up as then befitted a modest woman in public; now for him it tumbles down like a flock of goats cascading down a hillside (4:1). Verse 8 perhaps reflects her nervousness, so he invites her to leave her fears and descend into his embrace.

Here is a man delighting in his new bride. "You have stolen my heart, my sister, my bride" (v 9). We can only imagine what it felt like to hear these words.

Apply

If you're married, review how you speak to your spouse.

- ❓ *Do you praise his or her beauty and express your delight in their love?*
- ❓ *How could you do so more, or more tenderly? (And not just their physical beauty but their spiritual beauty too.)*

Sheep, towers… honey

It's easy to mock this husband's comparison of his wife's teeth to sheep or of her neck to a tower. Every culture has its own distinctive language for love. Future generations may find it strange that we name our loved ones after the viscous secretion of insects (i.e. honey). But perhaps our mockery is also a sign that we're missing the point. What is being described is a landscape. This is God describing his people, represented by their land.

Re-read Song of Songs 4:8-11, but this time read it as Christ's words to you. As you do so, leave your fears behind and descend into his embrace.

Pray

And now speak to Jesus in response to his words to you.

Consummated love

In these verses we reach the climax of the story and the song.

Him to her

Read Song of Songs 4:12-15

Throughout the Song, the bride's sexuality is likened to a vineyard or garden. Until now, it has been "a garden locked up" and "a sealed fountain" (v 12). In other words, she is a virgin who has not given herself away.

The description in chapter 4 has moved down the woman's body. In verses 14-15 it moves further down and becomes still more intimate. But there is nothing crude in her husband's description of her. Instead, the language becomes even more figurative, as if to hide her modesty. She is an orchard of fruits and spices, creating a profusion of scents that delight his senses (v 14).

Her to him

Read Song of Songs 4:16

For the first time on their wedding night, the bride speaks. She picks up his garden imagery and calls on the winds to waft her scents to entice her lover. "You are a garden", he said in verse 12; now she describes her sexuality as "his garden" and invites him to enter. "Do not ... awaken..." she said before their wedding (2:7; 3:5). But now she cries out, "Awake": "Let my beloved come into his garden and taste its choice fruits".

Time to leave

The time has come for us quietly to leave the lovers to their love-making. In 5:1 we switch from the present tense to the present perfect tense—we only return to their story after their love-making is complete.

Read Song of Songs 5:1

The middle point of the Song comes in 4:16 – 5:1. The woman's invitation to love and the consummation of that love form both the poetic and sexual climax of their story.

Apply

In Eden, humanity enjoyed an intimate relationship with God. Now, through the Song, we are again invited to re-enter the garden and enjoy Jesus, our Bridegroom. Not all of us are married; and of those that are, some of us are not happily married, and some of us are part of happy marriages that, for one reason or another, find sex difficult or impossible. So not all of us enjoy the sexual intimacy described in these verses. But the invitation to spiritual intimacy is extended to *everyone*. And this is not a second-best option because intimacy with Christ is the ultimate love to which human marriage and sex points. The application of these verses is for all of us to hear these words from Jesus: "Eat, friends, and drink; drink your fill of love" (5:1).

> ❷ *How will you pray in response to this invitation?*

Bible in a year: Lamentations

Longing

"The course of true love never did run smooth," said William Shakespeare. It was ever thus…

In 5:1, we see the consummation of the lovers' love. But we've not arrived at a happy-ever-after moment—not yet.

Read Song of Songs 5:2-8

❓ *Can you reconstruct the scene? What do you think is going on here?*

❓ *Can you trace this woman's emotions as the mini-drama unfolds?*

Perhaps he's arrived home unexpectedly. Perhaps she's not in the mood tonight. Perhaps it's simply late, and she's already tucked up in bed (v 3). Whatever the scenario, it's clear that his desires are frustrated. When he gets no response, he gives up (v 3-4). In the meantime, though, her desire has been aroused by his desire (v 4-5), but by then it's too late (v 6). When she can't find her beloved, she becomes reckless and "faint with love" (v 7-8).

Placing this episode immediately after the consummation of love in verse 1 is significant. Suddenly we lurch from climax to crisis. It's a reminder that human love is fragile and fleeting. Even the most intense moments of passion are soon over, and even the best marriages have their tensions.

The author and family expert Christopher West says, "God gave us sexual desire … as the fuel of a rocket that is meant to launch us into the stars and beyond". At the heart of human experience is longing—a longing that points us to fulfilment in God. As the 4th-century bishop Augustine famously said, "Our hearts are restless until they find their rest in you".

❓ *How do moments of romantic joy and sexual pleasure point us to God?*

❓ *How do frustrated longings and relational heartache point us to God?*

Apply

Even our experience of divine love can feel fleeting in this life. There are moments of intense joy, but they don't last. Think about your relationship with God.

❓ *Look back over recent months or years. Can you trace moments of great joy and times when your spiritual life felt flat?*

Both the highs and lows are meant to point us forward to the day when we see Christ face to face. The question is, when Christ comes knocking, can you be bothered?

❓ *How does this passage help you have a realistic and positive understanding of your relationship with Jesus?*

❓ *If you are married, how does it help you to navigate the ups and downs of your own relationship?*

Pray

Lord, may my desires lead me to you, and may my frustrations fuel my longing for your return. Amen.

Bible in a year: Luke 9 – 10

The unseen God

Out of sight, out of mind? David is exiled, a fugitive, far away from Jerusalem, where God's presence symbolically dwelled. But for him, the absence makes his heart grow fonder.

Thirsty for God

Read Psalm 63:1-2

❓ *What image does David use to describe his desire for God?*

❓ *Can you identify with that intense longing?*

TIME OUT

Psalms of devotion can be crushing. We tend to read them as a standard against which to judge our own faith. We then feel useless or doubt whether we are truly Christians at all. However, there is another way—a gospel way—to read them. And that is not as *pressure* but as *promise*. Psalm 63 doesn't set a standard of devotion that we must match; it shows us what is on offer in a relationship with God. We may not feel this way often now, but one day we will. God is preparing *joy for us*, and *us for joy* (Psalm 16:11), and the first half of this psalm gives a hint of what that will be like.

Delighted with God

Read Psalm 63:3-6

❓ *How does David describe his relationship with God here?*

❓ *How do these images help us as we think about what it means to be a Christian?*

Safe in God

Read Psalm 63:7-11

❓ *It's no surprise in this run of psalms to find David facing enemies. What does David do in the face of the threat (v 7-8)?*

❓ *What will God do for him (v 9-11)?*

⌄ Apply

Centuries later, in the middle of a hot, Middle-Eastern day, Jesus spoke to a thirsty woman at a well in Samaria. He promised her, and us, that no matter where we are, we can know "living water … welling up" in us as God's Son, Jesus, comes to live in us by his Spirit (John 4:1-26). The woman was filled with longing, and was seeking to satisfy it with romantic relationships. By offering himself as living water, Jesus teaches her, and us, that the soul satisfaction that we all crave is given to us freely in a relationship with Jesus Christ.

❓ *We're all tempted to look to other sources or relationships to satisfy that thirst for God. Where do you look?*

⌃ Pray

Pray that God would help you look for and find satisfaction in him. Pray too that when you feel empty, dry and thirsty as a Christian, you would not give up on God, but would cling to him and look forward to the day when we will enjoy God fully.

Bible in a year: Ephesians 1 – 3

Altogether lovely

Song of Songs 5:2-8 introduced the theme of unfulfilled longing. Now the friends prompt the woman to remind herself of why she loves her beloved.

Read Song of Songs 5:9-16

❓ *What's your favourite line in this rich description?*

The conclusion is clear: "He is altogether lovely" (v 16).

···TIME OUT····································

Read Revelation 1:12-18

❓ *What's your favourite line in this rich description?*

His mouth is sweetness

Re-read Song of Songs 5:16

We can't see Christ. But we can hear his voice when we read his word or hear it preached. Paul says, "The light of the gospel … displays the glory of Christ" (2 Corinthians 4:4). We see by hearing. We see the beauty of Christ when we hear the gospel message.

❓ *Recall some of the stories of Jesus in the Gospels. What do they reveal about his character?*

The conclusion is clear: Jesus is the "altogether lovely" one (Song of Songs 5:16).

We don't need to allegorise all the details of the description in verses 10-15. The point is that in the bride's eyes the beloved is altogether lovely. In the same way, when we look at Christ, we see one who is altogether lovely.

This is my friend

Re-read Song of Songs 5:16

There's no doubt that the lovers find each other physically attractive. But their love is more than skin-deep. They are also friends.

❓ *If you're married, are you cultivating a friendship with your spouse?*

❓ *If you're a Christian, are you cultivating a friendship with Christ?*

Read Song of Songs 6:1-3

Verse 2 recalls their sexual union in 5:1. He may be temporarily absent (5:6), but he's not permanently lost to her. What matters is that they're married, and therefore she belongs to him and he to her (6:3).

When Christ feels absent, we can rely on his covenant. He has promised himself to us. That covenant promise is confirmed and reiterated in baptism and the Lord's Supper. In baptism Christ says, *I am yours and you are mine,* and that mutual commitment is reaffirmed whenever we receive bread and wine.

🔼 Pray

❓ *Is there some characteristic of Christ that has caught your imagination today?*

If Christ feels distant, remind yourself of how he is altogether lovely. With this in mind, give thanks that you can say, "I am my beloved's and my beloved is mine".

Leviticus 1 – 3

You complete me

We sometimes talk about "feeling empty"—which raises the question: what truly fills you up?

Read Song of Songs 6:4-10

These verses echo the description of 4:1-3, but without its more erotic dimensions, perhaps because these are the first words of reconciliation after the break in relationship in chapter 5. Renewed sexual intimacy will come in chapter 7, once the relationship is repaired. Nevertheless the husband's desire is evident: her eyes "overwhelm" him (6:5).

Tirzah (v 4) was the original capital of the northern kingdom of Israel (until King Omri built Samaria), while Jerusalem was the capital of the southern kingdom of Judah. Once again, this description pushes us beyond the two young lovers to see God's desire for his people, represented by their capital cities.

King Solomon had 700 wives and 300 concubines (1 Kings 11:3). So Song of Songs 6:8 suggests this poem is set (though not necessarily written) while Solomon was still forming his harem. In contrast to Solomon's promiscuity, the Song affirms that true blessing is found in covenant fidelity to one person. This is true of both human marriage and our relationship to Christ.

Read Song of Songs 6:11-12

These verses are hard to interpret. If the garden is literal, then it seems to be the place where the lovers were reunited and reconciled. If it's figurative, then it's a reminder of sexual bliss. In either case, the husband's desires are fulfilled.

Read Song of Songs 6:13

There's no known place called Shulam. So "Shulammite" probably means "the woman of peace", because the Hebrew word for deep peace or contentment is "shalom". His wife is this man's "shalom-bringing woman", who makes him feel complete and content. Her name is a promise of desire fulfilled.

This is a reminder that God made humanity male and female, to be united in marriage, and that it's therefore "not good for [humans] to be alone" (Genesis 1:27; 2:18). But we also need to remember that human sexuality was created by God to point to Christ's relationship with the church (Ephesians 5:25-27. Written into the sex of our bodies is a reminder that we're ultimately only complete in Christ.

☑ Apply

❓ *What happens when we look to a human being other than Jesus to make us feel complete?*

❓ *Are you in any danger of doing this? How, and why?*

❓ *If you are married, how can you be a "peace-bringing" spouse?*

⌃ Pray

Is anything making you discontented or envious? Confess this to Christ in prayer and ask him to make you feel complete in him.

How he thinks of you

How do you think Christ views you? Why do you think that?

Perhaps you think he tolerates you. Or that he loves you because to love is the right thing to do, but you can't imagine he feels any affection for you.

Read Song of Songs 6:13

Let's have a look at her, demand the friends. But the man rejects their attempt to make his wife an object to be assessed or ranked. He will describe her beauty in 7:1-9; but to see it is for his eyes only. His love-making with her is not for public consumption.

▾ Apply

Job said, "I made a covenant with my eyes not to look lustfully at a young woman" (Job 31:1).

❷ *Do you need to follow Job's example?*

His desire is for me

Read Song of Songs 7:1-7

Beginning with the dancing feet of 6:13, the beloved moves up her body, delighting in everything he sees. He is captivated by what he sees. It's as if she's tied up his heart with her hair (7:5).

❷ *How do you think she felt when she heard this description?*

Read Song of Songs 7:8-10

Verses 8-9 are a statement of his intent to consummate their love in sexual union, and she welcomes his advances. He says her kisses are like wine, so she invites him to drink them in. Rejoicing in his desire, she gives herself to him in love (v 10).

The word "desire" in verse 10 is the word used to describe the curse of marital conflict in Genesis 3:16. In the couple's personal Eden, the curse is turned to blessing, for this is a loving, giving, intimate desire rather than a self-centred, wrestling sinful one.

Once again, we don't need to allegorise all the details of this description. The point is that in this husband's eyes his wife is beautiful, pleasing and full of delights (Song of Songs 7:6). And in Christ's eyes we are beautiful. He takes pleasure in his bride. He takes pleasure in you. He desires to love you and enjoy you in what older writers called "mystical union". His desire recreates the blessing of Eden.

▾ Apply

❷ *Do you hear the intensity of Jesus' desire for you? How will that change your view of yourself, and of your relationship with him?*

❷ *Will you seek to match his longing for you with a longing for him?*

Next time you pray or meet as a church or home group, don't ask yourself whether you got something out of it. Ask yourself, "Did Christ enjoy it? Did it satisfy his desire for his people?"

Come, let us go

"With my body I thee worship," say the old Anglican wedding vows.

Read Song of Songs 7:11-13

Throughout the Song of Songs, the woman's vineyard has been a picture of her sexuality. So verse 12 may be an invitation to see if she is aroused. If she is, then she will give herself to him in love. She will offer him "every delicacy" of love (v 13). This is her response to the desire he expressed in verses 1-9. Verse 12 may also be an invitation to see whether their love-making will result in fruit in the sense of children.

Apply

What is the proper response of the church to Christ's love?

Read Romans 12:1

❷ What does "proper worship" look like?

❷ How does God feel about us offering our bodies in this way?

❷ What is it that motivates us to offer ourselves in this way?

❷ What will it mean for you to use your body in this way today?

···· TIME OUT ··

Read Isaiah 5:1-7

❷ Israel, like the woman, is pictured as a vineyard. What does God find when he looks for fruit?

Read John 15:1-8

❷ How can we bear fruit for God?

Embraced

Read Song of Songs 8:1-3

Our singer wants to kiss her beloved all the time but obeys the constraints of public decency (v 1). So she leads him to the intimacy of her family home. The longing to be entwined in each other's arms which was expressed in the dream of 2:6 is now a reality.

Apply

In a lovely aside, we discover that the woman has learnt how to love from observing the example of her mother (8:2). We, too, learn how to love Christ from mothers and fathers in the faith (Titus 1:4; 2:3-5).

❷ Is there an older Christian who could mentor you?

❷ Is there a younger Christian whom you could mentor?

Reminded

Read Song of Songs 8:4

For a third time we are warned not to arouse love until it finds its true expression in marriage.

❷ Why might a reader (especially an unmarried one) need to hear this again at this point, do you think?

❷ In what way do you need to hear it?

 Bible in a year: Proverbs 4

Stronger than death

"Money can't buy me love," sang the Beatles. So, what is love worth? And how long does it last?

The flames of passion

Read Song of Songs 8:5-7

Death, the grave and fire are destructive powers; but love is their equal (v 6). Uncontrolled erotic love can wreak a world of harm. But within the constraints of marriage, it is a powerful force for good.

So these verses are both a warning and a promise. They reiterate the warning of verse 4: once awakened, illicit love cannot easily be contained or controlled. But covenant love promises a lifetime of joy "until death us do part".

To the church in our relationship with our Husband, this is a promise "that neither death nor life … will be able to separate us from the love of God that is in Christ Jesus our Lord" (Romans 8:38-39). The love of Christ is not just as strong as death; it is stronger than death, for his love defeated death when he died in our place on the cross and rose again in triumph. Even death cannot part us from him and his love.

Given and not bought

Read Song of Songs 8:7-12

❷ *What is the advice given in verses 8-9?*

❷ *What do verses 7 and 11-12 say about love and sex?*

Young people are to be protected from those who would use and abuse their sexuality (v 8-9). Love given away cheaply loses its value (v 7, 11; see 1 Kings 11:1-6). A woman's sexuality is something for her to give without coercion (Song of Songs 7:12).

In 1:6 the bride-to-be was shy and insecure; now in 8:10 she thrusts out her breasts in confidence. What has made the difference? His love. It is "his eyes" that have changed her view of herself (8:10). She has become his contentment—his shalom-bringing woman (6:13; 8:10).

Apply

❷ *What difference will the Lord Jesus' love for you make to you? What difference will knowing how he sees you make to your confidence today?*

Let me hear your voice

Read Song of Songs 8:13-14

In verses 13-14 the cycle begins again as the lovers renew their love-making, echoing what they have said before (2:9, 13-14). And today Christ comes to you to renew his relationship with you, and says, "Let me hear your voice".

Pray

Pray that the loving eyes of Christ would relieve your doubts and calm your fears. Thank him that whatever happens in this life and in death, he will love you.

JOEL: Worse to come

Here's the setting: an invasion of locusts has ravaged Judah, and the Lord has sent his prophet to tell his people how to respond to the disaster.

Joel is not dated, and we know nothing about the prophet beyond the fact that he was given this word from the Lord, and that he is the son of someone called Pethuel!

Read Joel 1:1-20

❷ *What images does Joel use in verse 6 to describe the locusts? How does this make us feel about the event?*

❷ *What are the effects of the disaster for Israel?*

This disaster points beyond itself to something else.

❷ *What does it point to (v 15)?*

Read 2:1, 11, 31-32; 3:18-21

❷ *What will happen on the day of the Lord?*

❷ *How does the locust invasion point to that day?*

···· TIME OUT ···

Read Luke 13:4-5

Jesus is teaching his listeners how to think rightly about a contemporary disaster.

❷ *What does Jesus not want his listeners to conclude?*

❷ *What does he want them to understand?*

❷ *What does he call them to do?*

❷ *How does this incident shed light on our passage in Joel?*

Note all the times in Joel 1 where the prophet tells the people how to respond to the disaster.

❷ *How should they respond; what must they do?*

This passage shows us that natural disasters serve to point beyond themselves to the greater disaster of the coming day of the Lord.

❷ *What are we to think and remember when we see disasters unfold? What is our right response?*

One of the most famous promises of the Bible is Romans 8:28: "And we know that in all things God works for the good of those who love him, who have been called according to his purpose".

❷ *In light of Joel 1, how can we see God fulfilling that promise to his people, in times of natural disaster?*

🔼 Pray

Think of one or two recent natural disasters. Pray that the Lord would use those events to remind you afresh of the coming day of the Lord. Pray that he would move you to repentance. Pray that he would renew your zeal for reaching the lost with the gospel, in light of that coming day.

Pray for those most directly affected by those disasters, and ask that the Lord would help them to respond by calling out to him.

The battle to come

The coming day of the Lord will be a "dreadful" day. God's purpose here is to call us to slow down and consider that reality very soberly.

From September to October 2024, a series of hurricanes caused major destruction to Florida's Gulf Coast in the USA. Hurricane Milton deposited so much rain over parts of Florida's Tampa Bay area that it qualified as a 1-in-1,000-year rainfall event.

The forecasters saw it coming, and their warnings in the days leading up to the storm were completely dire. They were clearly determined to make people sit up and take notice.

Joel 2:1-11 reads a bit like a weather forecast for a storm of apocalyptic proportions. And here the Lord seems intent on making us sit up and take notice.

Read Joel 2:1-11

Back in chapter 1, Joel told us about a disaster that had already happened. Now it seems that he looks forward to another disaster that is on the horizon for Judah. This one looks even worse. And like the first one, it points forward to the coming day of the Lord.

> ❷ *What are the hints in these verses that this coming disaster points beyond itself to the ultimate day of the Lord?*
> ❷ *What are the signs that an unrepeatable, world-ending disaster is coming?*

Joel uses a number of different images (including the image of the locust swarm) and separate scenes to paint a picture for us of that coming day.

> ❷ *How many different images and scenes can you find in these verses?*
> ❷ *How do you react to each image; how does each one make you feel? What does each one add to Joel's portrait of the day?*
> ❷ *What is the Lord's role in this coming disaster (v 11)?*
> ❷ *Is that a surprise to you? What does this tell us?*

Joel seems to be spending quite a lot of time and energy forcing us to slow down, and think about and imagine what the coming day will be like.

> ❷ *Why do you think he does that?*

⌃ Pray

Given that this day is surely coming, consider how you should be praying today for yourself, for your loved ones, and for others whom you will encounter in your community. Then spend time in prayer.

The right response

The Lord has warned us of a disaster that's coming. But now we see the purpose of his warning: to urge us to get ready, and so be spared.

The forecasters of the Florida hurricanes weren't just scaremongers. They wanted people in the path of the storm to take note and then get ready, preparing emergency kits and evacuating their homes where necessary.

Read Joel 2:12-17

There is a major change in tone between verses 11 and 12.

> ❷ *What is the Lord doing in verse 11?*
> ❷ *What is he saying in verse 12?*
> ❷ *What does it tell us about the Lord's character that he can issue the warning of verse 11 and the promise of verse 12 in the same breath?*

Joel doesn't give a specific reason as to why God is sending the disaster. He doesn't point to a particular sin that the Lord is addressing. But he does make it crystal clear how to respond.

From the heart

> ❷ *Which would be easier: "rending [i.e. tearing] your heart" or "rending your garment"?*
> ❷ *What is it about God and his character that makes it worthwhile to return to him?*

Joel doesn't quite give us a promise here in verse 14, but he holds out plenty of hope.

Sound the alarm!

The trumpet sounds in verse 15. It's as if a fire alarm has gone off in a public building—everyone needs to drop what they are doing and go. Just notice who is included in the call, and the things they need to stop doing.

> ❷ *Who is to speak to the Lord for the people?*
> ❷ *What will be the basis of their plea for salvation?*

Read Hebrews 7:23-28

> ❷ *Who speaks for us before God the Judge?*
> ❷ *What is the basis of his plea on our behalf?*

☑ Apply

> ❷ *Which particular areas of your life, and particular types of sin, has God been calling to your mind over the last few days as you have been reading Joel?*
> ❷ *What will it look like for you to return to the Lord "with all your heart" and to "rend your heart" before him?*

Why not spend some time in prayer, doing just that? And as you do so, rejoice that you have a High Priest in heaven who speaks on your behalf.

Better is to come

As God shows pity, the people are to celebrate his goodness. Natural disaster pointed to the coming day; now God's abundant provision points to the new creation.

A picture of the future

Read Joel 2:18-24

Back in verses 15-17, the people of Judah had gathered together in a "sacred assembly" and the priests had cried out to the Lord on their behalf. Verse 18 tells us that the Lord has heard the prayers of his priests.

When we cry out to the Lord for salvation from his judgment, we do so through our much greater Priest, Jesus himself.

> ❓ *In light of that, how is verse 18 an encouragement to you? What assurance does it give you?*
>
> ❓ *What motivates the Lord to respond in verse 18?*
>
> ❓ *What does the Lord do for this people in verses 19-24?*

The Lord even speaks to the animals in verse 22, to tell them not to be afraid.

> ❓ *What might that teach us about God's future blessings?*

The promise of physical blessing here seems to outstretch the historical experience of Judah. The description of the wilderness pastures "becoming green" in verse 22 echoes the description of creation before the fall in Genesis 1:11. (This is the only other place in the Old Testament where this exact language is used.)

Just as the disaster that Judah experienced pointed us to the day of the Lord, so too the blessing of Judah points us ultimately to the blessings of life in the new creation.

Adding to the picture

Read Revelation 22:1-5

> ❓ *How does this picture of life in the new creation remind you of Joel's? What does it add to Joel's picture?*
>
> ❓ *What insight does Joel 2:19-24 give us into life in the new creation?*
>
> ❓ *How do these verses teach and move us to respond to God's abundant kindness?*

⌃ Pray

Thank God that, through Jesus, he hears and responds to our cry for salvation.

Thank him for the hope of security and abundance of life in the new creation.

Pray that the joyful response of Joel 2:21 and 23 would be in your heart and on your lips today.

Locust compensation

God's promise of salvation is not just that his people will avoid judgment, or that it will be better in the future than it was in the past. It's deeper and richer than that.

The past

Read Joel 1:1-20

❓ *What was life like for the people of Israel when God sent disaster upon them?*

❓ *What did they suffer, and what did they lose?*

The future

Read Joel 2:24-25

❓ *How will things be different in the future?*

The people of Judah might have thought that the painful experience of chapter 1 was something that they simply had to write off. All they could hope to do was bury the memory and try to move on. But verse 25 suggests that those years will not be written off or forgotten. The Lord promises that he will "repay" his people "for the years the locusts have eaten".

❓ *So what should the people of Judah expect to happen in practical terms?*

You and I know the experience of pain and loss simply through living in a world under judgment.

❓ *As we look forward to life in the new creation, what hope does verse 25 give you?*

❓ *How does it help us to think about*

painful experiences (past and present) of living in this world-under-judgment?

No shame

Read Joel 2:26-27

Tomorrow, we will see that verse 28 points to the gift of the Spirit at Pentecost. Joel says that the gift of the Spirit will happen "afterwards"—that is, after the events of verses 26-27. That tells us that the promises of verses 26-27 must have been fulfilled before the day of Pentecost, at least in part (even if their ultimate fulfilment is yet to come in the new creation). And, of course, there has already been a major fulfilment of these verses—through the life, death and resurrection of Jesus.

The language of "shame" in the Bible often points to the shame experienced by those condemned on the day of judgment.

Read Romans 5:5-8

❓ *How do Christians know that their "hope" (that is, what they are trusting in) will not lead them to "shame"?*

❓ *How, according to Joel 2:26-27, are we to respond?*

🔼 Pray

Spend some time in prayer thanking God for the rich promises of these verses, and praising him for his great salvation in Jesus.

Getting the word out

One of the marks that God's salvation has arrived and that his judgment is coming is that God empowers his people to spread the news.

At train and underground stations in London, there are often people waiting at the entrance, handing out flyers for new restaurants and businesses. Sometimes they give out free samples or discount vouchers. Anyone starting a new venture knows that it's vital to get the word out.

God isn't selling anything, but he does have exciting news to proclaim. And he has enlisted help to spread the word.

Read Joel 2:28-32

In verse 28, referring back to the events of the previous verses—the arrival of the Lord's salvation—the Lord says that the things he is about to describe will happen "afterwards". That means that the events described in verses 28-32 will prove that his salvation has arrived.

> ❷ *So, what will be the proof that salvation has come?*

> ❷ *What else will these signs prove, or point to?*

The apostle Peter quoted these verses in his sermon on the day of Pentecost. To understand their significance, it will help us a great deal to spend some time seeing how he interprets and applies them there. After all, the best commentary on the Bible is the Bible itself! We will begin to look at Acts 2 today, and then continue tomorrow.

Read Acts 2:1-12, 14-21

> ❷ *How was the promise of Joel fulfilled on the day of Pentecost?*

> ❷ *How did the apostles and other Christians prophesy? (Hint: The word "prophesy" can mean different things in different places in the Bible, but at its heart, it simply means to speak God's word.)*

> ❷ *Why was the gift of the Spirit and the ability to prophesy a fitting (and very useful!) sign to mark the arrival of God's salvation, and to point to his coming judgment?*

> ❷ *What will this prophesying enable those who listen to do (v 21)?*

❖ Apply

If you are a member of God's people, you are a home of his Spirit, and you are empowered to spread the news of salvation and judgment.

> ❷ *How are you doing this? Do you need to do this more, or get started? To whom could you speak today?*

> ❷ *How will relying on the Spirit to empower you, rather than on your own abilities, change your confidence in evangelism?*

❖ Pray

Thank God that he sent Spirit-filled believers to speak the gospel to you. Pray that God might make you faithful and bold to speak the gospel to others. Pray that he might give you an opportunity to do that, even today.

Bible in a year: Proverbs 5 – 6

Signs with a purpose

Joel tells us that God's great work of salvation for his people and his coming judgment will be marked by dramatic signs on earth and in heaven.

Big events are often marked by big signs. If you are in a major city on New Year's Eve, you will know when the clock strikes midnight because fireworks will light up the sky. The sight of them will be unmissable. Here Joel shows us that the climax of God's work of salvation and judgment will be all the more unmissable.

Read Joel 2:28-32 and Acts 2:14-22

Joel promises that the arrival of God's salvation will be marked by wonders and signs.

❷ *According to Acts 2:22, when did those signs take place?*

❷ *What events in the life and ministry of Jesus might be included here?*

We often find it hard to know exactly what to do with the miracles of Jesus. What are they there for? Are they teaching us something? Should we expect to see similar miracles today?

❷ *Looking at the words of Joel as quoted in Acts 2, what were the "wonders and signs" in Jesus' life meant to show?*

Acts 2 is really still part of the introduction to the book of Acts, a book where we see how Jesus continued his ministry through his apostles.

❷ *How did the signs and wonders in the apostles' ministry support the spread of the gospel?*

Signs and wonders seem designed to dazzle and impress. But God's purpose is practical and serious.

❷ *Look again at verse 21. How are we and others meant to respond to the signs and wonders that Jesus performed?*

···· TIME OUT ·····································

Read 2 Corinthians 12:12

❷ *What do you think Paul means when he calls "signs, wonders and miracles" the "marks of a true apostle"?*

Read Hebrews 2:3-4

❷ *How do these verses reinforce what we've seen in Acts 2 and 2 Corinthians 12?*

◣ Pray

Praise and thank God that he gave us unmistakable proof that his salvation has arrived in Jesus and that the day of the Lord is coming.

Pray that you would have renewed assurance of the truth of the gospel as you look back to the ministry of Jesus and the apostles.

Good news of judgment

Now we zoom in to observe more closely God's work of judgment on that coming day. The picture is sobering for God's enemies, and comforting for his people.

Embarrassed?

It is easy to feel embarrassed about the Bible's teaching of judgment. There is so much good news to share: God's love for the world, the gift of his Son, his offer of grace. We are glad to tell our friends and neighbours about those aspects of the Bible's teaching; we are perfectly happy to sing about those things and praise God for them. But we find God's judgment harder to deal with or talk about.

It's easy to feel that way, but here in this passage the Lord wants us to see that his judgment of the world is very good news, and nothing to be embarrassed about.

Good news

Read Joel 3:1-3

❷ *How does the Lord describe the time of judgment (v 1)?*

❷ *Why do you think he describes it in that way?*

❷ *What have the nations of the world done?*

❷ *Why, specifically, is God putting the nations on trial (end of v 2)? What does that tell us about God's priorities and concerns?*

Read Joel 3:4-8

God suggests that Tyre and Sidon might be "paying [him] back" for something.

❷ *What have they done to him? How will he respond?*

At various points in the Old Testament, the people of Israel faced times of agonising suffering at the hands of foreign nations. The destruction of Jerusalem and exile in Babylon in the 6th century BC was one such time. The people might have been tempted to think that God had forgotten them, and that he was overlooking their suffering. But God has kept a careful record, and a day of reckoning is coming.

Today, God's people in different parts of the world are facing intense persecution, and many are being killed for their faith. It might be easy to think that God has overlooked his suffering people. But not a bit of it: he is keeping careful watch, and no crime against his people will go unpunished.

⌄ Apply

❷ *Why is God's judgment good news?*

❷ *Do you need to change the way you think, pray and/or speak about it? How?*

⌃ Pray

Praise and thank God for his loving concern for his people, and for his promise to judge.

Pray for believers facing persecution, and ask the Lord to uphold them in suffering and to help them to remain faithful to him.

Battle, harvest, refuge

In this passage, Joel paints a very sobering picture of the day of the Lord. It will be a day of battle and a day of bloodshed.

Certain defeat

Read Joel 3:9-13 and Revelation 14:14-20

In retrospect, it is quite clear that some great military battles of history were simply unwinnable for the losing side. Either the strategy was wrong, or the military might of the opponent was too strong. Here in these verses, the Lord invites the nations to join an obviously unwinnable battle against the ultimate superpower—God himself. It is a hopeless situation, but by the time of the battle, the world's armies have no choice but to participate.

❓ *In light of Revelation 14, who is the one exercising judgment?*

❓ *What will this day hold for the enemies of God?*

❓ *What reason does Joel give for God's judgment?*

Refuge provided

Read Joel 3:14-16 and Mark 15:33-34

Supernatural darkness in the Bible is often a sign of God's anger and his judgment. The darkness here reminds us that God is angry at the world's "wickedness" (Joel 3:13).

❓ *So what was the significance of the darkness that fell in the middle of the afternoon as Jesus died?*

Joel promised that "the LORD will be a refuge for his people" (v 16).

❓ *How does Mark 15 show us how God provided that refuge?*

Some of the most fascinating Cold War relics in the UK are the networks of nuclear bunkers that were built for key government officials to use in the event of a nuclear attack. Some were very sophisticated, with extensive catering and medical facilities. (One even had a BBC recording studio!) In the event of a nuclear disaster, the whole of the population would have been divided into two simple groups: those who had a place in the bunkers, and those who did not.

This passage reminds us that a day of disaster is coming in which the whole of the world's population will be divided into two groups: the Lord's people, who have refuge in him; and his enemies, who face destruction.

⌄ Apply

❓ *How do these verses shape and drive your priorities for non-Christian friends and family members?*

❓ *How do these verses help you to love Jesus more, to be more thankful to him, and to live more wholeheartedly for him?*

Thank God for refuge in Jesus, and pray urgently for the salvation of unbelieving friends and family.

 Bible in a year: Philippians 1 – 2

A glorious city

As he closes his prophecy, Joel takes us beyond the day of the Lord to give us a glimpse of life in God's eternal city, set apart for his holy people.

Many parts of London that were badly bombed in the Second World War were rebuilt in the 1950s and 1960s. Some architecture that looked cutting-edge then now looks pretty tired, and some of these areas have become known for crime and a range of social problems. In one such area, the local authorities have launched plans for a massive redevelopment. Demolition teams have come in and barricades have gone up. Massive posters show images of people sipping coffees in beautiful public spaces, outside beautiful new buildings, on a beautiful summer's day. The pictures depict a city of the future, presumably soon to take shape behind the wooden boards.

Here, Joel gives us a glimpse of God's city of the future—and it is very beautiful indeed.

Read Joel 3:17-21 and Revelation 21:1-4

Joel 3:17 makes us refer back to the previous verses.

❓ *Why will the events spoken of there show God's people that the Lord their God dwells in Zion?*

❓ *Now turn to Revelation 21. What city is Joel speaking about?*

❓ *What will the city be like?*

❓ *What will not be in the city? What is the future for other nations and other lands?*

Much of the book of Joel focuses on the day of the Lord, and acts as a warning to us to ensure that we are ready for that day.

❓ *Why do you think Joel ends as it does?*

···· TIME OUT ··································

If you have time, spend a few minutes reading through the whole of Joel again, jotting down the main things that God has taught you, the main challenges he has brought you, and the main encouragements he has given you.

❤ Apply

Joel has been speaking of God's salvation, now secured in Christ, and God's judgment, still to come.

❓ *What difference has his prophecy made to...*
- *your view of God?*
- *your view of your future?*
- *your reaction to hard things in your life?*
- *your witness to those around you?*

❤ Pray

Thank God for the sobering lessons in Joel about God's coming judgment. Pray that you would live in the light of that—fearing God rightly, and pointing others to his great salvation in Jesus.

Give thanks for this amazing vision of the future that God has in store for his people. Pray that you would delight in this prospect, especially in times of difficulty and discouragement.

Bible in a year: Leviticus 7 – 9 ❤

INTO HIS PRESENCE

Praying with the Puritans

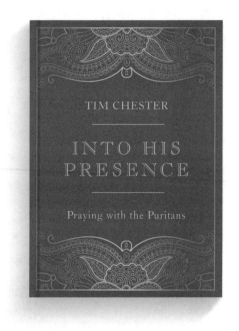

These biblical, warm and emotionally connected
prayers bring you the glories of Puritan spirituality
in an accessible form. Read in your personal
devotions or use to enrich public times of prayer.

thegoodbook.co.uk/intohis
thegoodbook.com/intohis
thegoodbook.com.au/intohis

THE LANGUAGE OF RIVERS AND STARS

How Nature Speaks of the Glories of God

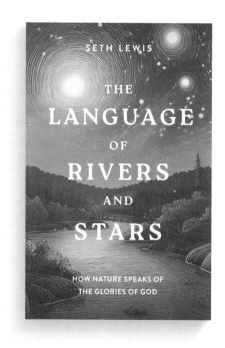

Being in the beauty of nature helps many of us to feel connected to God. Experience the gift of his creation in a deeper way as you use God's word to understand what he is saying to us through his world.

thegoodbook.co.uk/riverstar
thegoodbook.com/riverstar
thegoodbook.com.au/riverstar

Introduce a friend to

explore

If you're enjoying using *Explore*, why not introduce a friend? Time with God is our introduction to daily Bible reading and is a great way to get started with a regular time with God. It includes 28 daily readings along with articles, advice and practical tips on how to apply what the passage teaches.

Why not order a copy for someone you would like to encourage?

Coming up next...

- James
  with Sam Allberry
- Lamentations
  with Eric Schumacher

- Nehemiah
  with Stephen Witmer
- Acts 18 – 28
  with Matthew Hoskinson